NATIVE AMERIC

Quanah, Parker
One Man - Two Worlds

By
Carol Dean

ABOUT THE AUTHOR

My name is Carol Dean and I'm married with two adult children, and three grandchildren and we all live in the North East.

I started to write children's stories to entertain my children when they were young on rainy weekends or school holidays. My son writing stories about ghosts or vampires, and my daughter drawing pretty pictures. Nothing to do with the story but very pretty.

And this is where my *Granny Ridley* and *Charlie Dryden* stories first appeared.

Charlie Dryden's crime/adventure stories have since developed into an exciting series of books for 9-15 year olds. My funny *Granny Ridley* series for 7-10 year olds now has a further nine books. Plus *PC Polly*, my commissioned work, has since made an amusing addition for 7-10 year olds to have a good giggle over.

Many other characters have appeared and entertained various age groups, (adults included) in the shape of dinosaurs, spiders, teddy bears, a panda, unicorns, with a friendly ghost there too. I am delighted to say that my books are popular in many countries around the world. Literally worldwide which is brilliant.

All of which you can find out more about on my website www.caroldeanbooks.com or follow me on Facebook.

All rights reserved. This book or any portion thereof may not be reproduced or used in any manner whatsoever without the express written permission of the publisher except for the use of brief quotations in a book review or scholarly journal.

Copyright © Carol Dean 2021

According to the details that were detected, the images used in this book are free of copyright. Reasonable attempts to find licence owners of all images have been made.

Book cover images adapted from paintings by Henry F. Farny. Images used in cover:

- Lucky Shot   Main backdrop
- Hunter   The cut figure

ISBN: 979-8-70795-795-6

ALSO BY CAROL DEAN

GRANNY RIDLEY SERIES

- Granny Ridley Tries Exercise
- Granny Ridley Knows the Way
- Granny Ridley Goes on a Trip
- Granny Ridley in the Snow
- Granny Ridley and the Alien
- Granny Ridley Helps Out
- Granny Ridley Tries Knitting
- Granny Ridley Has a Weekend Away
- Granny Ridley and Wolfie
- Granny Ridley Gets the Runs

CHARLIE DRYDEN SERIES

- Charlie Dryden's Cricket Ball
- Help Me Charlie Dryden
- Charlie Dryden Finds a Bone
- Charlie Dryden and the Charnwood Abbey Ghost
- Charlie Dryden and the Guardian
- Beware Charlie Dryden
- Charlie Dryden and the Stolen Roman Standard

REAL FAIRY TALES

- The Real Cinderella Story
- The Three Bears and a Girl Called Goldie

DINOSAUR STORIES

- Spotty the Dinosaur
- Terry Comes Out of His Shell
- Spike Gets a New Sister
- Deano and the Baby Dinosaur
- Deano Has Lost His Roar
- Reggie Learns a Lesson
- Herbie's Big Day

STORIES FROM DAYS GONE BY

- Sophie the Suffragette

PC POLLY

- PC Polly the Police Lady
- Be Safe Be Seen PC Polly
- PC Polly on Patrol
- PC Polly and the Mini Police

GHOST STORIES

- The Day the Ghost Got Scared

CHRISTMAS STORIES

- Santa Steams Ahead
- Santa and the Magic Dust
- The Day Santa Met Santa

YOUNG READERS

- Peter the Panda is Hungry
- Webster Swings into Action
- Teddy Has Lost His Growl

MAGICAL STORIES

- Amelia Flurry and the Legend of the Unicorn

NATIVE AMERICAN SERIES

    Comanche Life
    A Man Called Sitting Bull
    Geronimo and Cochise – Two Apache Legends
    The Trail of Tears
    Quanah Parker: One Man - Two Worlds
    The Footsteps They Left Behind

WAR STORIES

    Ponsonby-Smallpiece - The Legend

You can find all Carol's books on her website www.caroldeanbooks.com.

CONTENTS

CYNTHIA ANN PARKER 1
NADUA 7
CYNTHIA IS KIDNAPPED (AGAIN)..15
QUANAH STARTS A LIFE ALONE 21
ADOBE WALLS 33
SURRENDER AND LIFE ON THE RESERVATION 42
QUANAH PARKER ONE MAN – TWO WORLDS 54
CATTLE BARONS AND FRIENDS 61
QUANAH'S DEATH 75
MEMORIALS AND LEGACIES 79
THE END OR THE BEGINNING?..83
ALSO AVAILABLE BY CAROL DEAN 91

FOREWORD

"Over this vast country, where for centuries our ancestors roamed in undisputed possession, free and happy, what have we left? The game, our main dependence, is killed and driven off, and we are forced into the most sterile and barren portions of it to starve. We see nothing but extermination left before us, and we await the result with stolid indifference. Give us a country we can call our own, where we may bury our people in quiet." Chief Ketumseh

A heart-breaking statement. One that affected many tribes of Native Americans over the many, many years that they literally fought to keep their lands. So that they could survive and continue to live as their ancestors had done before them.

I was only five years old, probably far too young to really understand, when my Grandfather gave me an encyclopaedia on the subject of **'Cowboys and Indians'**. My interest was piqued. It was a fascinating book and a huge insight into life as it was then,

But it was the true story of life then.

None of the John Wayne versions of clean cut nicely dressed cowboys, and the 'Indians' were always to blame scenarios. Although these were popular films at the time, particularly with my parents.

But it opened my very young eyes to the reality of it all and fascinated me more. This interest continued and became part of me as I grew up, with Geronimo being my hero alongside Sitting Bull and Cochise.

Then on a recent holiday visiting an Indian Trading Post, I found a photo of a very noble looking Native American. His wonderful face drew me to him and the photo became mine. He is ever present at home and I always promised myself (and him) that I would find out about his life.

That man is Quanah Parker. An amazing man. This is his story through me and it's my tribute to the Last Comanche Chief. **Quanah Parker: One Man – Two Worlds**.

QUANAH PARKER TIMELINE

I have also picked just a few of the dates from the list *(in bold Italics – please see end of timeline)* to show you what we in England were achieving on those particular timelines.

- **1836: Cynthia Anne Parker kidnapped**

- 1845: Quanah Parker birth year perhaps

- 1860: Battle of River Pease – Cynthia re-captured

- **1875: Quanah's surrender**

- 1877: Quanah successfully finds renegades for Mackenzie

- 1878: Buffalo hunt goes wrong

- 1884: Quanah arranges Comanche lands leased to cattlemen for grazing

- 1887: Dawes Act

- 1889: Jerome Act

- 1902: Quanah becomes Sheriff of Lawton

- **1905: Quanah attends inauguration of President Roosevelt**

- 1910: Quanah's Mother re-interred in Post Oak Mission Cemetery, Cache

- **1911: February 23rd Quanah dies**

- 1836: August – Midland Bank established in Birmingham as the Birmingham and Midland Bank

- 1875: August - Offences against the Person Act effectively raises the age of consent in England, Wales and Ireland from twelve to thirteen

- **1905: 12th May** – first public protest by suffragettes, led by Emmeline Pankhurst, at Westminster

- **1911: 31st May** – launching of the ocean liner RMS *Titanic* in Belfast

CYNTHIA ANN PARKER

Public Domain Image

Quanah Parker: One Man - Two Worlds

Cynthia Ann Parker

Cynthia Ann Parker was only nine years old in 1836 when she was kidnapped from the Parker Fort. By a band of Comanche. And Cynthia was one of the lucky ones.

The Parker clan had laid their roots and built themselves a fort with cabins, making it very fortified, and they had picked land that was right next to Comanche territory. This rather brave, or foolish, choice of land put them straight into American history books. Little did they know at the time, that what was to happen to them would be taught in American schools as part of history.

They were called the Parkers.

As a family, large though it was, they had all travelled from Illinois in the year 1833 with their worldly belongings in caravans pulled by thirty oxen. They had already been given grants of 4,600 acres of land near the present town of Mexico. Land that was given in perpetuity. No taxes for 10 years. A good deal?

Inspired by this wondrous land, they bought a further 16,100 acres, about 25.2 square miles. The Parkers were here to stay.

The land was magnificent. Trees for building, streams for fresh water, land to farm. Everything they needed. By 1835 there were two dozen people living there – six families of Parkers.

Public Domain Image

Quanah Parker: One Man - Two Worlds

Locals and government could not understand why they had chosen that particular location, and called them lunatic farmers. The Texas Republic had no resources to ensure that they were safe, so they really just washed their hands of them. Oklahoma was Indian Territory, and an extremely dangerous place to be.

And it was soon to prove how dangerous it was when a large party of Comanche, Kiowa (and possibly Caddo and Wichita - no one is really sure), arrived at the Parker fort on May 19th, 1836. What they found probably surprised them, as the very large secure gate of the fort was wide open. Well most of the Parker menfolk were working the fields, so why close the gate? The Native Americans were looking for food and water.

Patrick Feller from Humble, Texas, USA
https://commons.wikimedia.org/wiki/File:Old_Fort_Parker_Historic_Site_1708131329_(35797170354).jpg
Old Fort Parker Historic Site 1708131329 (35797170354)
https://creativecommons.org/licenses/by/2.0/legalcode

In her memoirs, Rachel Plummer, a young seventeen year old member of the family, pregnant at the time with her second child, wrote that **"one minute the fields (in front of the fort) were clear, and the next moment, more Indians than I dreamed possible were in front of the fort."**

A Native American approached the fort with a white flag, but no one inside the fort believed that the flag was a genuine gesture of peace.

As a rather late precaution, Silas Parker wanted the five men present in the fort, to take up a position on the walls and fight as best they could. Benjamin Parker, however, felt that by going out and talking to the Native Americans that he could buy some time for the majority of the women and children to flee out the small gate at the back. Or at least that was the hope.

Benjamin was also right in his thinking that the war party were determined to kill everyone in the fort, and they had probably already dispatched the unsuspecting men in the fields. He argued with Silas that they had to barter for their lives to make time for everyone else to escape. Silas reluctantly agreed with Benjamin.

Benjamin tried this but knew that it wasn't going to be a peaceful meeting. He sensed that he was in mortal danger from the Native Americans and according to Rachel Plummer's written account, Benjamin returned to the fort after his unsuccessful parley with the warriors, and told his brother and father that he believed they would all be killed, and that they should run swiftly to the woods.

But Silas seemed adamant that if they could just shut the gate and man the walls all would be well. Benjamin pointed out that there was no time and their **"course was decided."**

He told Rachel, **"run little Rachel, for your life and your unborn child, run now and fast!"** Rachel later wrote that he then went back outside.

Rachel apparently was, surprisingly, asked by Silas to watch the front gate, after Benjamin had gone out to talk to the Indians the second time, when she really wanted to escape as quickly as possible. Silas wanted to retrieve his musket and powder pouch. **"They will kill Benjamin,"** she reported her Uncle Silas saying, **"and then me, but I will do for at least one of them, by God."** At that moment, she said she heard whooping outside the fort, and then the Native Americans were inside.

Public Domain Image

Benjamin's bravery had bought them enough time so that the bulk of the women and children could get away. Rachel Plummer was afraid she would not be able to keep up while carrying her two-year-old son and being pregnant at the time would be a hindrance to running. Benjamin Parker was proved right and he was killed, and with the gates still open the rest of the Native Americans rushed inside.

Rachel began running after seeing the Native Americans come into the fort. She ran holding her little boy's hand, while behind her she said she saw the Native Americans stabbing Benjamin with their lances, and then she heard Uncle Silas shout defiantly as though he had a thousand men with him. But he too was soon dead. Rachel tried to get away, but she was knocked down and dragged off.

Elizabeth Duty Kellogg for some reason decided to go back and gather up their savings, $100 in coins, before she attempted to escape. A fruitless attempt I'm afraid.

Public Domain Image

Quanah Parker: One Man - Two Worlds

Public Domain Image

Samuel Frost and his son, Robert, were killed inside the gate, as they attempted to flee. John Parker's genitals were cut off and he was then scalped. His wife was left for dead.

Lucy Parker and her youngest two children were initially captured but were rescued by David Faulkenberry, a family member, as he ran up to the fort from the fields where he had been working. Her two oldest children, however, along with Rachel and her son, and Elizabeth Kellogg were kidnapped.

In all, five men were killed, some were left for dead, two women and three children were captured, and the rest escaped into the wilderness.

Rachel Plummer's account of her capture is horrific. She 'skirts' over many aspects of her capture too dreadful to write about, and details the outcome of those kidnapped children.

One of those children was Cynthia Ann Parker. History was in the making.

NADUA

Public Domain Image

Nadua

Cynthia Ann Parker was one of the lucky ones. Her kidnapper was the Chief of the Nokoni band of Comanche, and she was adopted into the tribe as the foster daughter of Tabby-nocca.

As to the rest of the family, their lives were cut short after much maltreatment. Treatment that Cynthia would have witnessed at such a tender age. But she still was one of the lucky ones.

Cynthia's 'adoptive parents' had only just recently lost a child of their own and this was something that the Comanche and other tribes did. Kidnap a white child, bring it up as your own, and if the child assimilated well they stayed. If not then they would be sold on to another tribe or back to the white man. Or worse.

But Cynthia Ann, being so young, settled quickly and was given the name Nadua (foundling or someone found), and she loved her life with the Comanche.

Being as young as she was helped her to be assimilated into the tribe very quickly, as she learnt their ways, learning the language and becoming a very good worker. And she had many a chore to learn as the women in the tribe did everything, cooking, mending, skinning, moving camp, setting up camp, as well as bringing up any babies to.

So having an extra pair of hands would prove very useful. Especially if that someone was willing and able to help other females complete their chores and had a really good hand at intricate decorative work for clothing and tipis. Over time she became a valued and respected member of the tribe.

Public Domain Image

When she grew into a woman and became old enough in Comanche eyes to marry one of the tribe, the Chief's son Peta Nocono (**he who travels alone and returns**) gave many horses to have her as his bride. A happy marriage it appeared to be, and her life was a joy for her.

She loved the life, as hard as it was for a woman, and she adapted to it so well. She was happy.

The camp that Nadua now lived was located near the Pease River, which originates in the Texas Panhandle and wends westward along the northern corridor of Texas and joins the Red River. The country was pretty and vast. Wide, high prairie plains were broken by the river and the hills and the steep ridges that rose from the creek.

Public Domain Image

Life for a Comanche woman was a very busy one and Nadua's days were now filled with tasks. Particularly after a buffalo hunt when she and the other women of the camp would start the very hard work of dismantling a possibly fifteen-hundred-pound buffalo, or maybe even more than that, to work on.

This was always women's work, as was almost anything to do with a buffalo that did not involve tracking it and killing it.

Once the beast had been slaughtered the Comanche women had to cut the meat into strips for drying ready for their various food staples like pemmican. Absolutely everything was used. They would have a process to tan the hides and make their clothes, or repair tipis. Plus harvesting the paunch which could end up as water bags or cooking pots, they used sinew for sewing, the marrow from bones and even the ground-up brains became useful to soften the hides. Every scrap of these huge beasts was the used. It's how they existed and they only killed for food.

Public Domain Image

What Nadua and the other females had to do was bloody, messy work and I would imagine disgustingly smelly too. It's hardly surprising that they would spend most of their time covered from head to toe in buffalo fat, blood, marrow and tissue. So much so that it turned her Nadua's naturally light hair and light skin almost black.

It would have been really hard to spot her as the white woman in the Indian camp. But having already had many an offer of horses in exchange for Nadua a fearful Peta Nocona would often blackened her face with ashes or make her hide away. Buying and selling captives was usual with Comanche, and a trader called Williams offered 12 mules and 2 mule's worth of merchandise for Nadua. Williams was told by Peta Nocono that he would *"rather die than give her up"*. I think it must have been a happy marriage.

Public Domain Image

Her work as a Comanche woman continued, and while she worked, she watched her children. She had three children now. Quanah being the eldest of them.

Quanah is said to have had very fond memories of his mother, his baby sister Prairie Flower (Topsannah), and his younger brother Pecos (meaning Peanuts, named because Nadua could remember eating peanuts by the fire when she was small).

Although Nadua had to share her husband with a full blood Comanche woman, Peta Nocona was a good provider and she too enjoyed her status as the wife of a prominent war chief. I suppose in Comanche terms, as he had many horses, they were rich.

Public Domain Image

Quanah's birth year is really unknown, but it is said to have been about 1845. It really depends on what you read and who has written it. Admittedly even Quanah himself couldn't remember when it was.

Being the son of a powerful war chief, a man with much influence and many horses and a talented hunter, Quanah had more privileges than the other boys of his age, although Comanche boys were allowed a lot of freedom and did not have to perform menial tasks.

Depending on the weather, Quanah would have gone naked until he was about nine years old. After that he wore a breechclout, leggings, and moccasins. The leggings often had fringe work, a trademark of the Comanche. In winter he would wear a heavy robe made from a buffalo that had been killed in the late fall, when the creature had grown a dark brown winter fur that was up to twenty inches thick. Envied by many a white man due to their ability to keep their wearers lovely and warm, and much better than a blanket.

Public Domain Image

Comanche boys, Quanah included, would be experts at roping and catching horses, and riding successfully since the age of about four years old. From that point onward Quanah would have spent an enormous amount of time in the saddle. His horse would quickly become an extension of his physical being. It was the Comanche way.

But Quanah also needed to be taught the secrets of weaponry, usually by his grandfather or another elderly male.

Archery, both from horseback and on foot, was something the Comanche excelled at. From fifty yards a warrior could reliably hit an object the size of a doorknob four out of five times.

As a boy approached puberty, life quickly became more serious as the skills he needed in hunting, survival and fire making, would become very useful to him in a very short time to come. This was the life and all these skills were necessary if you wanted to survive and be an important member of your tribe.

With puberty too came the vision quest where the boy became a man in the eyes of the tribe. Each boy on the quest would have four things: a buffalo robe, a bone pipe, some tobacco, and material for producing fire. On the way to the vision quest site, often a hill or a warrior's grave or some other special place, the boy would stop to smoke the pipe four times. During the four-day quest the boy would fast.

Over the four days and nights, the idea was for the young brave to remain in this chosen place until he received a vision.

We do not know exactly what the result of Quanah's vision quest was. Later he told of dreaming of a bear. So therefore his medicine as an adult was bear medicine, which meant that the bear was the source of his power, his puha.

Despite coming from a mixed marriage, Quanah somehow looked totally Comanche and I expect that he epitomised exactly what a white man would have thought a noble 'savage' would look like.

He was described as **'a large, long-limbed boy, much taller and stronger than the average Comanche. As an adult he was a strapping six-footer, nearly a head taller than many of his peers. In later photos the sheer mass of his biceps and forearms is apparent.'** Sounds impressive to say the least.

He was already a superb archer and an accomplished hunter. As a youth, and as a warrior, he became known for his **'careless, daredevil sort of courage, quite in contrast with the stealthy, deadly character of Indian warfare'**.

He was also described as **'extremely intelligent, forthright, aggressive and fearless'**. Traits that showed from a very early age.

But in October 1860, events were to change the course of history for the United States. It would not be long before Abraham Lincoln was elected as President, even less time before the US was split apart politically and the blood of a million men would be spilt in the American Civil War.

But none of this was apparent to Nadua, her family or the Comanche.

The Comanche were aware that the white man was moving ever closer and they worried that this impact could alter the course and the supplies of game in their hunting grounds. But they continued their lives despite this living their lives on the plains just as they had done for centuries.

But life was soon to change for Nadua and her family very, very quickly, and it was out of anyone's control, and ended up being bloody.

CYNTHIA IS KIDNAPPED (AGAIN)

Public Domain Image

Quanah Parker: One Man – Two Worlds

Cynthia is Kidnapped (Again)

It seems unbelievably sad that Nadua was enjoying her life with her Comanche husband and children and unbeknown to them all, it was about to be decimated.

Her marriage is reported to have been a happy one, but in December 1860 it changed momentously, when Quanah's mother was recaptured (or kidnapped again), along with his little sister, by the Texas Rangers led by Lawrence Sullivan 'Sul' Ross. It was called the Battle of River Pease.

Public Domain Image

Not only were Nadua and Prairie Flower taken away, but it was reported that Peta Nocona was killed (facts are vague) and Quanah and Pecos just managed to get away with their lives escaping alone. Quanah was still a young boy and was never to see his Mother or sister again.

It was an extraordinary feat for Quanah, not only elude to capture by the Texas Rangers, but also to be able to care for his younger brother Pecos at such a harrowing time.

Quanah already had the skills to survive. With these skills he was able to look after himself and Pecos, hunting small game to keep them alive, and making fire when it was needed and safe to do so.

16

Quanah, despite all the odds, was able to follow the tracks of the Comanche band members who had escaped the battle with their lives, and catch up with them without bringing down the wrath of the Texas Rangers pursuing him. One of the Texas Rangers was in fact a young man called Charles Goodnight, who would meet up with Quanah again much later, and form a friendship with him.

Charles Goodnight – Texas Ranger

The Texas Rangers in the meantime having successfully saved a white woman who had been searched for years, took Nadua and Prairie Flower back to Fort Cooper and contacted her family - the Parkers. They lived in Birdville Texas.

This was not a success. Nadua was Comanche now and pined for her husband and sons and would not assimilate back into the white man's world causing much upheaval and upset in her newly re-found family. Her aim was always to escape from her captors, and she tried many times unsuccessfully.

Her story and her existence is a very sad one. She was a curio to the people not only in her family, but wherever she went because she was a 'white squaw'. She had lived with the 'savages' and had become a 'savage' herself. This was something to see, and they were happy to pay for it too.

Nadua was always tied up in just case she tried to escape again, and put on display where everyone could come along and stare at 'the white squaw', the tears streaming down her face. Sometimes she was just tied up outside a local store, so that people could gawp at her in wonder. Many, many, times she tried to escape back to her family, the Comanche, and many, many times she was dragged back to the bosom of her 'real family'. The Parkers. They tried to make her more like them, the women of the family, bathing her and dressing her in fancy clothes. She hated the all the female clothes they made her wear and craved her buckskins.

Despite their efforts, with Cynthia being very sturdily built about five foot seven inches tall, making her a giant amongst the Comanche women, and weighting about one hundred and forty pounds, it was impossible to make her look like a typical woman of the time wearing a dress. She had her hair cropped short, very blue eyes and a look of anger or perhaps defeat set on her face.

Many a time she removed her white man's clothing as she tried to run away. She would rather be naked than wear the garments they made her wear. She hated the white man's food and sometimes did without that too.

Prairie Flower was very young at the time of the re-capture. She was described as *'a sprightly child. Dark skinned and strikingly pretty. Everyone liked her'.* Prairie Flower had already started to accept the white man's ways learning the language and going to school. But sadly she became ill with one of the white man's diseases (influenza and pneumonia) and died in 1864, leaving Nadua totally alone. Nothing from her life with the Comanche was left. So she had nothing to live for and she too died in March 1871 of influenza complicated by starvation.

But her story lives on in American history still today as it is taught in many of their schools.

Public Domain Image

So much so that the John Wayne film *'The Searchers'* comes from Nadua's story.

Natalie Wood played the role of Cynthia Ann although it was a different name in the film (Debbie Edwards and John Wayne played the Uncle

Ethan Edwards). But in the film despite Ethan Edwards wanting to kill his niece because of what she had become, a savage, he relents when he sees her and takes her home. Happy ending.

Public Domain Image

But it wasn't like that in real life. Traders would often have stories of seeing a white woman or child with Native Americans as they traded, so many rescues were attempted and successfully made. But bringing the women from Native American camps and then returning them to their families wasn't always a good thing.

You would think that this was the right thing to do. Get them away from their captors. But it really was so wrong. Some may have wished to return, but once reunited with their families life was not so good.

Returned captives had a truly bad life on their return. If they had been married before their capture their husbands didn't want them back. Not after they had been living with 'savages'.

If they were single when captured, then again no one would want to marry them. They had lived with 'savages'. ***"Goodness only knows what those savages had done to those poor women,"*** would be the usual response from a family faced with the return of a loved one. But they still didn't want them back in the arms of their family again. ***"The embarrassment of it all. What would the neighbours think?"***

The women soon became lepers of society. Ignored and hidden away by their families to save more embarrassment. Or sometimes sent on their merry way to find their place in society, as long as it was a long way away from their family.

Quanah Parker: One Man - Two Worlds

Some turned to prostitution. No one cared then. Not their problem any longer. Some didn't stay long in the world which probably made it easier for their families to accept. ***"She just couldn't live with the shame of it all."***

They probably would have had a better off staying with their Native American captors.

But **'The Searchers'** is a good film and makes you think about how things were in those days and the hugely difficult choices that a family had to make after such traumatic upheaval. And the massive impact on the females involved.

Such was Nadua, Cynthia Ann's plight and her ultimate end.

QUANAH STARTS A LIFE ALONE

Public Domain Image

Quanah Starts a Life Alone

After the Battle of Pease River, Quanah's life changed dramatically. The comfort and status of being a chief's son vanished immediately. He had gone from being the son of a powerful war chief, a man with much influence and many horses, a talented hunter. Now he was an orphan.

Comanche culture that did not accommodate orphans. At first he was cared for by his father's Comanche wife, but she died within the year, leaving him and his brother with no near relatives to care for them. **"We were often treated very cruelly,"** Quanah apparently said later.

Then Pecos died too of unknown causes. Quanah was left alone. **"It then seemed to me that I was left friendless,"** he reportedly recalled. **"I often had to beg for my food and clothes, and could scarcely get anyone to make or mend my clothes. I at last learned that I was more cruelly treated than the other orphans on account of my white blood."**

In spite of this hardship, Quanah became a full warrior when he was fifteen years old.

Public Domain Image

After Peta Nocona's death Quanah joined the Nokoni band where the head Chief called Kiyou (Horseback) took him under his wing, training Quanah to be a considerable warrior as he grew up. Quanah soon left and joined the Quahadi (Antelope Eaters).

At this stage most Comanche warriors often took a more active masculine name in maturity, but Quanah retained the name his mother had given him, initially as a tribute to her after her capture.

The other thing that distinguished Quanah in the years after the Pease River Battle was his intense hatred of the white men. **"He wished to avenge the wrong,"** his son Baldwin Parker had written later. **"He understood, too, that white people were responsible for his father's death."**

And Quanah did exactly that for many years, stealing much needed horses and food supplies from mule trains as they entered the Comanche lands. Taking revenge with white man's lives too.

Public Domain Image

But everything had changed so much that it was now harder to go blindly adventuring about the American southwest in search of horses and supplies. Comanche power was still strong and still dominant but it was no longer unchallenged, as many forts had been built along the San Antonio–El Paso trail just to make sure that the wagon trains were protected from attack, but also to disrupt or even stop any Comanche raiding party coming into Mexico.

Fort Stockton was one of those forts, built near the site of the much needed waters of Comanche Springs, one of the largest springs in Texas. The water hole was an important landmark.

Now because of the fort the water was almost unobtainable to Quanah and his fellow braves, which meant that they could go without water for days. Even the Mexican settlements were now heavily fortified and armed ready for any attacks. Life was getting harder for the Comanche.

Many a time they came back from raids without having had any success. There would be no victory dances held in their honour sadly.

If he hadn't been so young and carefree and enthusiastic about his life, he might have noticed that things were beginning to change and that this would have an impact on the Comanche. But this was to come later in his life.

Public Domain Image

But the US Government kept up their attempts at making peace treaties with the Comanche, mainly to get them off the land and into reservations. Peace treaties that were reneged so many times by the white man and a document that Quanah would never, ever sign.

He was witness at one such event. The Medicine Lodge Treaty.

An enormous amount of energy was spent making pointless treaties with Comanche and many other tribes. Adding to the list of already failed treaties by the US Government.

One historian has estimated the number of treaties made and broken by the government at 378. The outcome of nearly every treaty was the same. White civilization advanced, Native American civilization was destroyed, or pushed out.

In October 1867, at a campground where the Kiowa held medicine dances, about seventy-five miles southwest of the present site of Wichita, Kansas, a peace treaty meeting was held. It was known as Medicine Lodge Creek.

Public Domain Image

The participants were members of the US Peace Commission and representatives of the Comanche, Cheyenne, Arapaho, Kiowa and Kiowa Apache tribes. The conference was the last great gathering of free Native Americans in the American West.

It ended up to be one of the biggest events arranged for a peace treaty, but it was doomed from the start, as peace treaties were. Nine American newspapers were invited along to cover the proceedings, with the US Peace Commission and William Tecumseh Sherman, the head of the army in the west, arriving with a huge wagon train of people and supplies. All in the aim to 'out do' whatever the Native American could do.

Public Domain Image
General Sherman

But they also brought along a mounted guard of five hundred soldiers in dress uniform, dragging their lethal, snub-nosed mountain howitzers behind them. What kind of message did that send to the Native Americans I wonder?

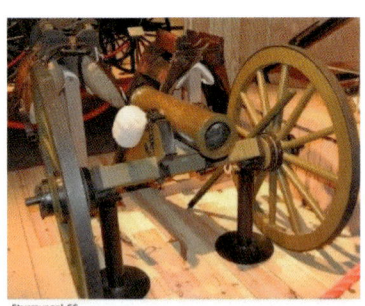

Sturmvogel 66
(https://commons.wikimedia.org/wiki/File:M1841MtnHow.png)
M1841MtnHow https://creativecommons.org/licenses/by-sa/3.0/legalcode

With an estimated four thousand Native Americans attending, including one hundred Comanche lodges, the food supplies had to be replenished very quickly with supplies of fifteen thousand pounds of sugar, six thousand pounds of coffee, ten thousand pounds of hard bread and three thousand pounds of tobacco. Luckily the mobile kitchens brought along could cope with the demands for food.

The meeting provoked a huge show of strength from either side, one trying to 'out do' the other as you would expect. Trying to look more fierce or stronger than the other. But when it got down to the 'nitty gritty' of the treaty it turned out to be just the same as all the others.

Sherman told the Native Americans present they would have to give up their old ways and learn to become farmers. And there was nothing, they were told bluntly by the man who was a notorious fighter, that they could do about it

One unknown Chief is said to have said, *"When I was in Washington the Great Father told me that all the Comanche land was ours and that no one should hinder us in living upon it. So, why do you ask us to leave the rivers and the sun and the wind and live in houses? Do not ask us to give up the buffalo for the sheep. The young men have heard talk of this, and it has made them sad and angry. Do not speak of it more."*

But the response was not what they wanted to hear, *"You can no more stop this than you can stop the sun or the moon,"* Sherman said. *"You must submit and do the best you can."*

And so they did, signing what is reported, amounted to '*a gigantic abstraction that was based on notions of property, on cartography and westward migration, and on the larger idea of Manifest Destiny, none of which they would ever completely comprehend.*'

The Native Americans were naturally unhappy about what they were being asked to do. It meant loss of land, loss of freedom, and loss of traditions. But it appeared that they could do nothing about it and many of them decided that it seemed far better to agree with the white man yet again with a treaty (especially one that came with gifts attached) than to refuse and therefore unleash warmongers like Sherman.

On October 21st, 1867, chiefs from all of the tribes put their marks on the treaty, which of course they could not read.

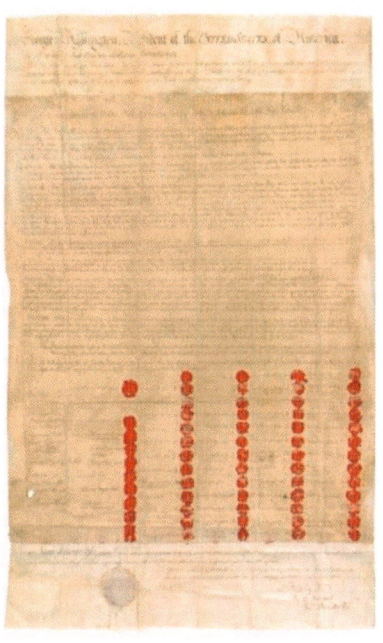

Public Domain Image
Source: National Archives and Records Administration

They included headmen from the Yamparika (Ten Bears, Painted Lips, Hears a Wolf, Little Horn, Dog Fat and Iron Mountain), the Nokoni (Horse Back, Gap in the Woods) and Penateka (Silver Brooch, Standing Feather).

The Quahadi, as a band, had never signed anything, and never would. But that did not matter to the US peace commission as they decided in their wisdom, that as the numbers were great and the signatures many, they had all the signatures they needed. The treaty was a done deal.

Amongst the Quahadi was the young warrior, Quanah. Why he was there is unknown but he had been staying in a Cheyenne village and heard that this big pow wow was happening and that food would be brought in vast quantities.

Quanah's own description of this pow wow is said to be, *"I went and heard it,"* Quanah said later. *"There were many soldiers there. The council was an unusual one, a great many rows. The soldier chief said 'Here are two propositions. You can live on the Arkansas and fight or move down to the Wichita Mountains and I will help you. But you must remember one thing and hold fast to it and that is you must stop going on the warpath. Which one will you choose?' All the chiefs decided to move down here [to the reservation]."*

Public Domain Image

This meant that their life as they knew it would be over and they would have to conform to the white man's ways. It was signed but they could not have understood the implications of having to share a 2.9 million acre reservation in what is now south-western Oklahoma, between the Comanche and the Kiowa.

It was good land admittedly, with plenty of hunting and good water sources, and it was located in Comanche territory and included Medicine Bluffs and other sacred sites for the Comanche.

Public Domain Image

But it was a tiny fraction of the Comancheria, Comanche lands, which at its peak held nearly 200 million acres. Nor did it include by far the richest of the old hunting grounds, the Texas bison plains.

Public Domain Image

The Cheyenne and Arapaho southern bands, agreed to live on a reservation, which convinced some Comanche that perhaps they too would be better off on the reservation.

On June 30th, 1869, it was estimated that there were 916 Comanche on the reservation, but none of them were self-supporting farmers like the white man. They were still living their way in tipis and hunting.

Reservation supplies from the US Government were sporadic and unreliable, so they had to do something. The Comanche then developed a routine of arriving and camping on the reservation and to claim other food and annuity goods during the winter months, then leaving in springtime to hunt buffalo or raid the Texas frontier. But Quanah continued raiding.

In 1868 Quanah became involved with raids from the camp in the Llano Estacado. The leader was a chief named Bear's Ear.

Leaflet (https://commons.wikimedia.org/wiki/File:Llano_Escarpment.jpg)
Llano Escarpment, https://creativecommons.org/licenses/by-sa/3.0/legalcode

Between 1868 and 1872, Quanah was now attached to the Quahadi, a band that seems to have developed out of the Kotsoteka in the 1850s.

But before any raids happened councils were held. Chiefs like Hears the Sunrise, who was a chief of the Yamparika (the Yap Eaters), whose domain was traditionally above the Canadian River and Milky Way, a Penateka chief who had chosen not to go to the reservation with the rest of his band. Many different bands were now coming together in their fight against the white man.

One of Bear's Ear's ideas for a raid was to strike hard at the ranches and farms in the area of Gainesville (fifty miles north of Fort Worth), gathering many horses. White settlers were probably killed at this raid but nothing is said to be recorded.

They got as far as the Red River when they were attacked by a force of soldiers that had been dispatched from Fort Richardson (near Jacksboro) to find them. A bloody fight followed, during which Bear's Ear was killed.

Usually, once the Chief has been killed in battle that means that his 'great medicine' has failed and the rest of the warriors stop fighting, and the white man has then won. Again usually the Native Americans would normally collect the chief's body and go back to camp leaderless and rather unhappy after a fruitless battle.

But not this time. With Bear's Ear being killed, Quanah took the opportunity to continue the fighting. **"Spread out,"** he is said to have shouted to the warriors. **"Turn the horses north to the river."** This was totally different to Bear's Ear's plan.

With Quanah urging them on, the Comanche warriors turned the herd and raced over rough ground toward the river. Quanah was followed by a bluecoat, who shot at him. Instead of running away quicker, Quanah turned his horse round and confronted the soldier head on.

He then charged, as did the soldier, both with their weapons at the ready.

The soldier fired his revolver and his bullet grazed Quanah's thigh. Quanah's arrow, meanwhile, found its mark in the man's shoulder. The soldier dropped his weapon, turned his horse, and fled.

Public Domain Image

But Quanah was now easily targeted by the other soldier's fire so he dropped down behind his horse in the old Comanche way, and, with bullets singing all around him, raced after his own war party. Somehow they managed to get their stolen horses over the river and back to their camp safely. They were not pursued by the soldiers, and that night there was huge celebrations and the tribe chose Quanah as their leader.

But this was just the start of his warrior career. Quanah's outstanding bravery on the battlefield meant that he became, at a very young age, one of a small, select group of Comanche men who would lead the tribe's final raiding and military expeditions in the last years of their freedom.

But the numbers of Comanche were actually dwindling. It's reported that there were perhaps about four thousand Comanche, out of which only one thousand had refused to move to the reservation.

The one certainty was that, in spite of considerable government effort, Comanche remained Comanche.

They had not and would not be broken from their old habits and traditions.

ADOBE WALLS

Kim Douglas Wiggins
https://commons.wikimedia.org/wiki/File:Second_Battle_of_Adobe_Walls_Study.jpg
Second Battle of Adobe Walls Study
https://creativecommons.org/licenses/by-sa/3.0/legalcode

Quanah Parker: One Man - Two Worlds

Adobe Walls

In 1873, a man called Isa–tai, claiming to be a medicine man, came into Quanah's life.

Public Domain Image

This man, aged around 23 years old, claimed to have miraculous healing powers and that he could raise the dead. That was very strong puha something that the Comanche had never heard of before. Puha is a mystical or magical power. We might say 'mojo'.

Although Isa-tai had never been in battle, he claimed that the white man's bullets would not harm him and that he could also 'make medicine' that would make the rest of the tribe safe from the white man's bullets too.

All were impressed and when Isa-tai called for all the bands of Comanche to gather and perform the Sun Dance (a Kiowa tradition) they did just that, such was his power. Only this time in the Sun Dance they discarded the rite of the warriors' having their skin pierced on the chests and thongs attached whilst hanging from the lodge pole. This to some of the tribes was an essential part of the Sun Dance. But they decided that on this occasion they would have a simpler version of the dance with much feasting, drinking and of course drum beating.

They gathered in May on the Red River site and Quanah and Isa-tai used the gathering to recruit new warriors for revenge attacks into Texas.

Other Chiefs present among who were Isa-Rosa ("White Wolf") and Tabananika ("Sound of the Sunrise") of the Yamparika, and Big Red Meat of the Nokoni band, had other ideas for raids. Their suggested an easier option of attacking the buffalo hide traders/hunters at a particular trading post, as this trade in hides was decimating the buffalo and the Comanche only real source of food supply. They were trading in a place called Adobe Walls.

One of the elders is alleged to have said to Quanah, **"You pretty good fighter, Quanah, but you not know everything. We think you take** pipe first against the white buffalo hunters. You kill white men and make your heart feel good. After that you come back and take all the young men and go to Texas war path. Isa-tai make big talk that time. [He said] God tell me we going to kill lots of white men. I stop the bullets in gun. Bullets not penetrate shirts. We kill them like old women."** The decision was made and the first target became Adobe Walls.

Kim Douglas Wiggins
https://commons.wikimedia.org/wiki/File:Second_Battle_of_Adobe_Walls_Study.jpg
Second Battle of Adobe Walls Study
https://creativecommons.org/licenses/by-sa/3.0/legalcode

It was agreed Quanah and Isa-tai would lead about 700 warriors from Comanche, Kiowa and Cheyenne, all totally motivated warriors believing Isa-tai's claim that his medicine would stop the white man's bullets, they headed off to the trading post, Adobe Walls. And they all trusted, or they would not have been there, that Isa-tai had true puha, and that they were immune to the white man's bullets.

But it didn't really work out as well as they had hoped.

Adobe Walls was a basic fortress housing a store and corral, a sod saloon (dug into the side of a hill or made from whatever material were at hand) owned by James Hanrahan, a blacksmith shop (Tom O'Keefe) and a sod store used to sell or purchase buffalo hides, all of which served the population of 200-300 buffalo hunters in the area.

Public Domain Image

The trading post at Adobe Walls was made of two foot thick sod walls, and nothing that the Comanche literally threw at them would penetrate that kind of thickness. Also take into account the weaponry that the buffalo hunters used in the long-range .50 calibre Sharps rifles.

But somehow the saloon keeper knew that the raid was going to happen and he kept his customers from going to bed by offering them free drinks.

Public Domain Image

In the early hours of the morning of June 27th, 1874 the attack happened. But despite the Native Americans getting really close enough to bang on the doors and windows, the fight was not an easy one.

Billy Dixon inside Adobe Walls recalled that **"At times the bullets poured in like hail and made us hug the sod walls like gophers when an owl is swooping past."**

This is Quanah's own account, of the battle through the interpreted words of his friend J. A. Dickson:

"We at once surrounded the place and began to fire on it.

The hunters got in the houses and shot through the cracks and holes in the wall.

Fight lasted about two hours.

We tried to storm the place several times but the hunters shot so well we would have to retreat. At one time I picked up five braves and we crawled along a little ravine to their corral, which was only a few yards from the house.

Then we picked our chance and made a run for the house before they could shoot us, and we tried to break the door in but it was too strong and being afraid to stay long, we went back the way we had come."

They needed to move back and gain some cover from the white man's rifles which they did.

Firing at Adobe Walls as they retreated, Quanah's horse was shot out from under him at five hundred yards. He hid behind a buffalo carcass, and was hit by a bullet that ricocheted off a powder horn around his neck and lodged between his shoulder blade and his neck. The wound was not serious, and Quanah was rescued and brought back out of the range of the buffalo guns.

Public Domain Image

Isa-tai tried to lessen the blame on himself by saying that the dreadful defeat at Adobe Walls had come about because his magic had been 'weakened' before the battle when one of the Cheyenne violated a sacred taboo by killing a skunk. The Cheyenne took offense to this and Isa-tai received a severe beating, was discredited and publicly humiliated.

But this defeat did not stop Quanah reeking revenge at every opportunity on the buffalo hunters and any white man that got in the way.

"I take all men, go warpath to Texas."

Attacks were made as far north as Medicine Lodge in Kansas. The entire frontier targeted. Stages were attacked, stations were burned, and hide men were tortured and killed. Men were staked out on the prairie and murdered in terrible ways. That was the law of the land. Had it been the white man, he would have inflicted similar tortures too on the Native American.

It's recorded that during that summer an estimated one hundred and ninety white people were killed and many more wounded. But it had exactly the outcome that Quanah was looking for. It stopped buffalo hunting in its tracks.

Hunters and settlers and anyone on the edge of the frontier fled to the protection of the federal forts for their own safety.

Public Domain Image
President Grant

Public Domain Image
General Sherman

Retaliation came swiftly from the US Government as on July 26th, 1874, when Grant gave Sherman permission to order the army to move immediately and in force to stop the Comanche once and for all. And they had permission to use whatever tactics or force that was required. No limits. No bars. Just do it!!!! Just kill them all.

Returning to the reservation and saying you were sorry would gain the Comanche nothing. It was too late for that now.

The bluecoats were now, as the notorious warrior Grant put it simply and bluntly when he said, **'to subdue all Indians who offered resistance to constituted authority'**. The plan, for which an enormous amount of army firepower would be brought to bear, was to hunt them all down.

This deadly decision led to Ranald Sliddell Mackenzie leading a victory with his 4th Cavalry and his Tonkawa scouts when they destroyed a Comanche village at Palo Duro Canyon on September 28th, 1874. Mackenzie's initial target was Quanah who was emerging as a dominant figure in the Red River war clashing repeatedly with Ranald Mackenzie.

Leaflet (https://commons.wikimedia.org/wiki/File:Palo_Duro_2002.jpg)
Palo Duro 2002 https://creativecommons.org/licenses/by-sa/3.0/legalcode

He had found Quanah's trail. And with 46 companies of US army Infantry and Cavalry, about 3,000 men he had the largest force ever dispatched to hunt down and destroy 'Indians'.

But Quanah managed to avoid and evade all of Mackenzie's attempts and this went on for months. Mackenzie must have been tearing his hair out over this one Comanche. So Mackenzie decided to try a different tactic.

The only way to strike at the heart of the Comanche was to remove their food and also their horses which was their wealth. Mackenzie located the Comanche village and totally destroyed it. Both Comanche and soldiers were killed but some of the Comanche managed to escape. But only just. They had nothing left.

Then Mackenzie took the decision to destroy 1,500 Comanche horses and destroy their wealth. It was a gruesome job, and it took time.

Mackenzie ordered his men to rope the horses together and lead them to face firing squads. As more and more horses were killed, they became harder to handle. It resulted in a massive pile of dead horses. Perfect horses slaughtered.

These dead animals were left to rot in Tule Canyon, and eventually turned to bleached bones over the years, becoming a very gruesome landmark. A grotesque monument marking the end of the horse tribes' dominion on the plains. Eventually some enterprising person gathered what was left up and sold it for fertilizer.

Mackenzie's slaughter of the Comanche horses also started a legend. It is said that on certain nights, a phantom herd can be seen galloping through the canyon, rider-less, their ghostly manes flying in the wind. I can believe it.

The Comanche had nothing left. No food, no shelter, poor clothing, and now they had to walk as their horses had gone. Some managed to escape and eventually turn up and surrender at the Fort Sill reservation in Oklahoma. There was literally just Quanah's band of the Quahadi left.

In a later interview, it is said that Quanah confirmed that he had in fact spent the fall and winter playing hide and seek with the US Army. **"Having several hundred good horses,'** he said, '**we kept a good watch for the approach of the enemy, and when we would learn that** *they were coming in our direction we would quickly move. Several of my men, with our families, kept up that kind of tactic all winter . . . During that time we were almost continuously going, as the soldiers were after us and many times they were almost upon us."*

They hunted buffalo when they could, but food was scarce and they had to resort to the old Comanche 'stand by' of eating nuts, grubs and rodents. It was a very bad time for the Comanche.

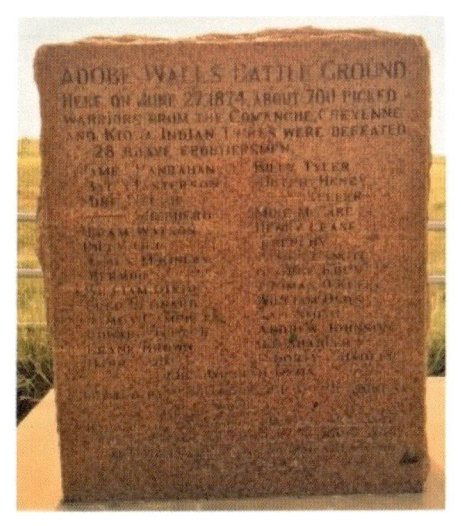

AZGUNZ
https://commons.wikimedia.org/wiki/File:Adobe_Walls_Battle_Ground_Names.jpg
https://creativecommons.org/licenses/by-sa/4.0/legalcode

Quanah Parker: One Man - Two Worlds

SURRENDER AND LIFE ON THE RESERVATION

Public Domain Image

Surrender and Life on the Reservation

Things were not looking good for the Comanche and Quanah knew this. There was really only one thing to do and that was gather everyone together and decide the next move.

A pow wow was arranged, and both Quanah and Isa-tai, surprisingly as Isa-tai had lost favour due to the outcome of Adobe Walls, were among those present.

Isa-tai is said to have said of Quanah, *"he is no chief but admits that he has much influence over his people – he has not acquired this influence by being a warrior and what influence he has he has acquired by kind treatment of his people, never abusing them. He has a big heart, loves everybody and every living thing that he never gets mad or strikes even a beast."*

And during this pow wow Quanah, although he still had an intense hatred for the white man due to the capture of his mother and the death of his father at their hands, could still see that surrender was possibly the only option.

It's said that Quanah had a vision whilst meditating about this dilemma praying to the Great Spirit for guidance. He saw a wolf that ran off in the direction of Fort Sill, and an eagle that swooped down several times before flying off. All this was enough to convince Quanah that he was being advised to surrender.

His people agreed and on May 6th, 1875 they all headed towards Fort Sill, despondent, half-starved as the winter had been severe. It took them until June 2nd, 1875 to arrive at the Signal Station a few miles away from Fort Sill. A ragged, tired and defeated group of four hundred and seven Quahadi, surrendered themselves, their horses and their weapons to the US Army there.

Life on the reservation had begun.

Ranald Slidell Mackenzie was already in post at Fort Sill, and his interest was piqued as soon as Quanah arrived. Not for any vengeance, as they had battled with each other for some time, but because he admired the man and the Quahadi.

Oklahoma and Indian Territories map

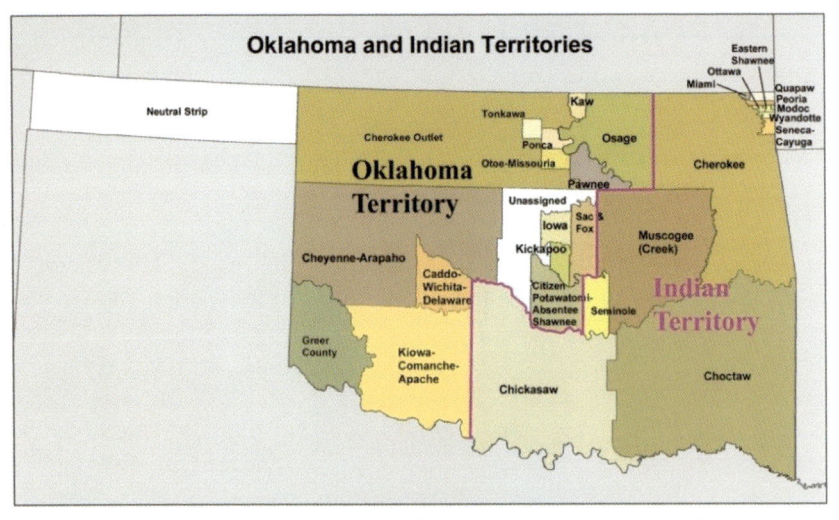

anonymous (https://commons.wikimedia.org/wiki/File:Okterritory.png), „Okterritory", https://creativecommons.org/licenses/by-sa/3.0/legalcode

When he learned they were coming in, he wrote to Sheridan: ***"I think better of this band than of any other on the reserve . . . I shall let them down as easily as I can."***

And he did.

The Quahadi were allowed to keep a few of their remaining horses, and he made sure that no one in Quanah's band was held as prisoners in the icehouse or guardhouse at Fort Sill.

But Mackenzie's interest in Quanah ran deeper than this as he had already discovered the identity of Quanah's mother, and had written a letter to discover the whereabouts of his mother and sister too.

The letter was also published in a Dallas newspaper, and information was found that both Quanah's sister and his mother were dead.

He had not yet met Quanah, and already he had rather unpleasant information to give to him who, at this stage, was a famous Comanche Chief. But it was to be the start of a lasting friendship over the years.

Quanah Parker: One Man - Two Worlds

Public Domain Image

But Quanah like the rest of the Quahadi had arrived at the reservation just like many others, poverty stricken, starving and having to stand, like everyone else and wait in line for their meagre rations.

When Quanah arrived at Fort Sill he had two wives, a daughter, although highly thought of by his people, he like the other had very little to show for it, and it just didn't seem to matter anymore,

As it happened Quanah was only one of a number of chiefs with a claim on band or tribal leadership. There were older leaders like Horseback (Nokoni), Milky Way (Penateka), Shaking Hand (Kotsoteka), Wild Horse (Quahadi) and most especially Hears the Sunrise (Yamparika), all of whom had more influence than Quanah did.

Reservation life was never going to be good. Quanah knew this from the onset. The reservation system was both cruel and humiliating, the 'taibos' (white men) had taken everything away from them and gave very little in return. The promised food and clothing was either scarce or of very poor quality that it was unusable. But they were now dependent on this to survive.

They ended up being dependant on the Bureau of Indian Affairs for food, clothing and shelter. Since the Comanche had moved to the reservation, they not only had to face hunger and poverty, but the white man began illegal takeovers of their land. Discriminated against and destitute as a tribe, they still struggled to maintain their traditions. Their traditions of hunting food for themselves had gone as there was no game on the reservations. They were stuck there with no hope and no future. It was a prison.

They were allotted goods which were classed as an annuity for the Comanche/Kiowa tribes amounting to $30,000 of axes, frying pans, tin plates, butcher knives, thimbles and some form of clothing, made from very cheap materials and all in one basic size. Children were not given any allocation of clothing so the women had to cut down the adults clothing to fit, then use anything left over for children's clothes.

Public Domain Image

Home

A lot of the allotted goods were worthless. Just rubbish really. But these second rate items had to be distributed to the Comanche and the Kiowa tribes. About 3,000 people which meant the grand total of $10 per person (roughly $251.37 in today's dollars). The Comanche sold theirs on to white men.

Their meat ration was issued 'on the hoof' and they were allocated 1.5 pounds per person per day. But even this proved to be a disaster.

It was assumed by the US Government, that the beef would be healthy and give fine beef rations, but perhaps if they had good grass to eat they might have been. But these animals had lost so much weight that they were just walking hides.

But every week from a large fenced off area (corral), it would be announced which of the tribes turn it was to 'hunt' the 'steer' (ration cows). The animal would then be released and 2 - 3 Comanche warriors, whooping and yelling, would chase and kill the animal with their bows and arrows and sometimes pistols. Once the animal was killed it would be skinned and divided up for everyone.

The rest of their meagre diet consisted of the rationed non-beef items (flour, coffee, sugar and salt). Again discrimination as these promised supplies just didn't turn up every week, and they were much less than soldiers rations, which meant families went hungry rather a lot. Or they had to eat very poor quality goods. Any horses or mules that the Comanche did have left became part of their diet, just to stay alive. Either that or starve.

The Comanche had to change their lives to protect themselves, and all this depravation became the motivation and turning point for the brilliant, influential and successful man named Quanah. The man who came to hold the title of the last Chief of the Comanche. And he had plans.

Quanah knew that something had to be done and had begun to understand that any power to change this had to come from the white man. Only the white man could appoint leaders and that's what Quanah needed to be to help his people.

With this in mind Quanah developed relationships with the Indian agent, the Quaker J. M. Haworth, and the army commander, Colonel Ranald Slidell Mackenzie.

Mackenzie had already discovered the fate of Quanah's mother and sister and he had to tell Quanah this. Quanah must have been devastated as now his hopes and dreams of meeting them again were now shattered. All he could do to honour his Mother was to add the name Parker to his. He then became known as Quanah Parker.

Flickr: Creative Commons
Licence/Commercial Use Allowed

But Quanah knew that somewhere out there he had a white family, the Parkers, and with help, continued to contact them via letter.

Although an extremely bright individual, (Quanah could speak English, Spanish and obviously Comanche), Quanah's level of literacy altered with the way he was feeling at the time. He could sound very intelligent and his dictated letters/words would show. But sometimes if he didn't feel like it, he would revert to speaking very basically as if he didn't have much understanding of English. Possibly a bit of Quanah humour there too.

His relationship with Mackenzie continued to develop rather well inspiring Mackenzie to write a letter to Cynthia Ann's eighty two year old Uncle Isaac Parker in Fort Worth on Quanah's behalf.

In it, Mackenzie wrote that Quanah was upset that the Parkers wouldn't accept him into the family, and pleaded Quanah's case by saying Quanah **"certainly should not be held responsible for the sins of a former generation of Comanche, and is a man whom it is worth trying to do something with."**

Sadly Isaac Parker apparently did not reply.

But reports state that this did not halt the friendship between Quanah and Mackenzie developing between the two men. They lived quite close to

Quanah Parker: One Man - Two Worlds

each other although Mackenzie's abode was rather nicer in Fort Sill's officer quarters while Quanah was in a tipi.

Quanah was a very keen learner and Mackenzie was apparently very happy to help him learn. Quanah wanted to know the white man's ways, and being a 'quick learner' he was soon complimented on his manners and began to be trusted by others too. Being a 'people person', a sociable person, he began to fit in well. The Comanche are sociable people and add this to his skills of thinking laterally and motivational skills too, then he was quite a leader.

He liked people and people liked him, simple as that. He'd motivated many warriors when needing help in battle. Now he had to hone those skills to motivate his people into the white man's world. Slowly his people started to listen and follow him as his reputation as a leader, encouraging them to take the white man's path and try farming. He succeeded and gained a lot of trust from the 'powers that be' running the reservation.

Proving his ability came quite quickly on the reservation as many Comanche still craved their old life. So off they went buffalo hunting without permission to leave the reservation.

Quanah knowing full well that, if caught by the white man, this could lead to their deaths, volunteered to bring them back and he was trusted enough to be given this task. And he succeeded.

Flickr: Creative Commons Licence/Commercial Use Allowed

Quanah Parker: One Man - Two Worlds

On the reservation the Indian agent (Haworth), to try and make supply distribution easier, divided up the tribes into 'beef bands'. He chose leaders that he felt he could trust from each of the bands, and by 1878, Quanah had been named head of the third largest band. He was a Chief now. The Principal Chief, and as it happens he was also the last Chief of the Comanche.

But he was also a 'boss'. He was **"a trusted, forceful, resourceful and able leader."** The white man approved and trusted him, and that meant that he had power. Power he could share with his people.

He could now control and distribute rationed goods fairly. He was a man with power. White man's power. But it caused problems for him initially as some of the other Comanche leaders did not like the way he was now important in the 'taibos' (white man's) world, and showed their dislike for him because of it. It made his life awkward on the reservation, but not awkward enough to stop him from trying to improve the lives of his people.

As Quanah had already proved himself to be trustworthy he was again given another retrieval task by his friend Mackenzie. Another group of Comanche had left the reservation with their families and Mackenzie wanted them back within the confines again.

So Quanah headed off during July 1877 with a very small band of two older Comanche men, three women and a few US Government mules to carry their supplies.

In order to ensure their safety, Mackenzie had written Quanah's mission in great detail on army letterhead should they be stopped. It said that Quanah had permission to be away from the reservation and his efforts had not to be interfered with. It was a good job really as the territory Quanah would be travelling on was still a very dangerous place to be. Particularly if a white man (buffalo hunter) spotted a small band of Comanche, then shooting would happen quite quickly. They would have been easy prey. It was a dangerous mission.

But Quanah wasn't looking for a battle. He was on a rescue mission. No war. No battle. Quanah was a different man now. But still a feared man I would have thought. Notorious especially out there on the Plains.

Being back on the grasslands of the plains must have been a rather enjoyable experience even if Quanah was on a rescue mission for the white man. It was summertime but that was fine for the Comanche. They were used to the heat during that time of year.

But a group of forty black soldiers from the Tenth Cavalry led by Captain Nicholas Nolan was also out in the severe heat of the plains looking for the same band of 'renegades'. Renegades because they had heard that they had attacked buffalo hunters, and Nolan wanted them caught and brought to justice. Justice being swift and deadly.

Comanche and Kiowa's had long been uneasy about black troops, whom they called 'buffalo soldiers' because of their tight, curly hair which reminded the Comanche/Kiowa of a buffalo's ruff. They considered 'buffalo soldiers' as bad medicine and were the only enemies that they would not scalp because of their tight curly hair.

When they encountered Quanah and his small band they immediately stopped them and Quanah produced his covering letter from Mackenzie. The content of the letter was not good news for Nolan, but Quanah being such a cooperative and helpful person, told Nolan that he thought he knew where the 'renegades' were and was heading that way himself. This information inspired Nolan to head off quickly in the direction indicated by Quanah to get there first.

Trouble was Quanah had told a bit of a porky here, and watched happily as the cavalry headed off in the wrong direction.

But Captain Nolan so determined to get to the 'renegades' first didn't think about the conditions that he and his cavalry would encounter on the plains. His provisions were sadly inadequate for the heat of the summer.

Things got so bad for them that they had to resort to drinking their own and their horses' urine. Mixing it with sugar apparently makes it taste better. I for one will take it as read. You can try it if you want to. They managed to survive and strangely enough didn't find the runaways. Funny that.

Quanah, on the other hand, found them straight away camped on the Pecos River and over the next few days had discussions with them to convince them to return to the reservation.

"Quanah told us that it was useless for us to fight longer, for the white people would kill us all if we kept on fighting," wrote Herman Lehmann, a former captive who had become a full-fledged, battle-hardened Comanche warrior and who was among the renegades. ***"If we went on the reservation the Great White Father at Washington would feed us, and give us homes, and we would in time become like the white man, with lots of good horses and cattle, and pretty things to wear."*** (On August 26th, 1901, Quanah Parker provided a legal affidavit verifying Lehman's life as his adopted son 1877–1878.)   Wikipedia

This may sound like another white lie from Quanah, as he knew exactly what reservation life was like. But they had no reason to disbelieve him. The main thing is it worked and they agreed to return peaceably with Quanah and his band, and they may have not got off as lightly had they been found by Captain Nolan. They definitely got the better of the deal.

Quanah and his little band escorted them back over the same dangerous territory (about 250 miles) returning to the reservation on August 20th with fifty-seven Native Americans (probably no more than fifteen fighting men) and one white captive (Lehmann) into the reservation, travelling by night for safety.

Mackenzie was impressed. No bloodshed, and everyone was brought back safely. He allegedly praised the young chief's **'excellent conduct in a dangerous expedition'.** Taking a chance on how well Mackenzie did actually feel about him, Quanah then persuaded Mackenzie and the Indian agent Haworth not to send the runaways to prison. And they weren't. This gained him the gratitude of the tribe too.

Public Domain Image

Another 'feather to his cap' was the proposed merging of the Kiowa-Comanche agency with the Wichita agency. This would mean a huge journey of around fifty miles for the Comanche just to get their meagre rations. In his role as the acknowledged leader, he spoke for his people and how he opposed the move. They listened and changed the plans for the merger. Success.

But Quanah had even more plans.

Public Domain Image

Although Quanah and his people had accepted and were now well on the white man's path, Quanah was still a Comanche at heart.

It wasn't just Quanah that felt this way either. Even though they had adopted many of the white man's way there was just one thing that he would like to do. One more time.

He lobbied to be allowed to go on one more buffalo hunt. To ride on their lands again, reliving their past, to be unsupervised, and away from the reservation. Just this once. And they were allowed.

QUANAH PARKER ONE MAN – TWO WORLDS

Public Domain Image

Quanah Parker One Man – Two Worlds

His lobbying had worked. They were going on a buffalo hunt. It must have felt marvellous to gain permission to hunt again on their wonderful lands just like the old days. In March 1878, a small band of Comanche/Kiowa men, women and children left the reservation for the hunt.

But their joy turned to anger very quickly when all they found were slaughtered carcasses of dead buffalo, killed by the hunters for their hides and tongues, and left to rot. It was tragic.

Public Domain Image

They travelled for miles but it was the same everywhere. Dead carcasses.

Quanah could not believe that this could have happened. That he was witnessing the decimation of what had been their supply for food, clothing, lifestyle and traditions just rotting away. It must have been devastating.

But good did come out of this although it was some time later. Quanah with his sharp business like mind soon found a solution to yet another hurdle that the Comanche had to tackle. A new future for him and for the Comanche as a whole.

But at the time, he was unaware that cattle herding was now big business and the actual cattle trail led right through the heart of the Comanche-Kiowa Reservation in Oklahoma.

And the man behind this big business was a man called Charles Goodnight (a Texas Ranger who tracked Peta Nocono, Quanah's father). He was now the proud owner of Palo Duro and one of the richest and most prominent ranchers around giving his name to its main cattle trail

'The Goodnight-Loving Trail' (Loving referred to Oliver Loving, his business partner).

Charles Goodnight - Rancher

Out of probably total frustration and upset, Quanah and his band started to slaughter the beef roaming on the canyon for food. Charles Goodnight became aware that this was happening very soon and, very bravely, rode out to meet up with Quanah and his band.

Naturally he wanted to know why Quanah and his band were killing his beef and Quanah answered him very simply. Goodnight was on Comanche land and as there were no buffalo left, they needed food and the beef would have to do.

The discussion, through an interpreter came to a really good conclusion. And that was that Goodnight would give him 'two beeves' every other day until they found buffalo. A successful parley and a peaceful one too.

This successful parley between the two men also started a friendship and mutual respect that would last. Plus Goodnight's help started Quanah on the road to becoming a businessman himself. Goodnight was apparently given the name of 'Leopard Coat Man', and school children in Texas have to study the agreement between Quanah and Goodnight as part of their history curriculum. Amazing.

Truthfully speaking there was no law that said the white man could not use Comanche reservation lands. So they did as the cattle trails had lush grass which meant that the cowboys running the cattle would stop on the reservation lands to fatten up the herd, and they could be there for weeks at a time. No one was going to stop them, but Quanah did see a way for the Comanche to gain from this. And they did.

Public Domain Image

Cattle herding was now big business. In order to be part of this Quanah developed small groups of Comanche, not war parties, who would actively 'police' the areas of the reservation used by the cowboys.

One cattle herder who is said to have encountered these 'police' and although they did not attack, they had made their presence felt. Quanah was there and approached saying, *"Your government gave this land to the Indian to be his hunting ground. But you go through and scare the game and your cattle eat the grass so the buffalo leaves and the Indian starves."* Quanah gained six fat cows that day. A peaceful battle but a battle won.

Quanah then came up with a toll payment for the cowboys and their cattle charging fees of $1 per wagon and 10 cents per head of cattle. Once the fees were paid the cattlemen were then protected by Quanah's men while they were crossing the reservation. That 'protection' included instructions on where to travel to find the best water.

The cattlemen that refused the 'protection' still paid but quite differently, and I don't mean with violence. I mean their cattle reduced in numbers as a payment. Those who did not cooperate made payment in other ways. One outfit reportedly lost 295 head to the Comanche on a single drive. I bet they paid the next time round.

This little bit of commerce grew with Quanah being given a job by one of the big cattle barons and he earned $35 a month. Quanah could also see that this was also an opportunity to lease out the unused grazing lands to the white man. More money for the tribe.

Public Domain Image

Not everyone agreed with his business drive as some Comanche and Kiowa could only see this as a bad idea as it could encourage the white man just to take the land from them. Quanah saw this as a good money making opportunity for the Comanche to make money and build their own herds. And it was.

His quest took him to Washington quite a few times to plead the Comanche case on this matter. After all he was the Principal Chief of the entire Comanche nation and a diplomatic representative for all the other tribes on the reservation. He was a resourceful and very able leader to perform this. His trips were probably paid for by the cattle barons anyway as they too were keen for the leasing agreement to be approved.

But it was worth all the effort as he won the fight in 1884, and the unused grazing land was leased to cattlemen. But only cattlemen that Quanah approved of like Samuel Burke Burnett and W. T. Waggoner. He did have opposition from 'Hears the Sunrise' (Tahbaynaneekah) about the land and wanted Quanah to have his authority as a tribal leader removed. It didn't happen.

Quanah Parker: One Man - Two Worlds

Public Domain Image

A deal was agreed at six cents per acre per year on a six-year lease. Which later increased to ten cents an acre.

On top of this deal Quanah secured roles for fifty four Native Americans to be hired by cattlemen, giving them the opportunity to learn the 'ropes' which would help with the steadily growing herds of cattle that Quanah was starting to amass.

His business head led him to investing money from the leased land into railroad stocks, and he became a wealthy business man. Probably the wealthiest Native American business man at that time.

Although he was now well established in the white man's world wearing suits and owning his own car, he never forgot his roots and continued to wear his hair long and in braids under is Stetson hats, and for comfort he preferred moccasins to boots. That proud Comanche was still there.

Public Domain Image

Quanah Parker: One Man - Two Worlds

During the reservation time the Ghost Dance appeared and was suddenly becoming a trend on the Comanche/Kiowa reservation at Fort Sill.

It's a religious ceremonial practice that some Native Americans believe that the dance would drive away the white man and that buffalo would come back. Sadly the dance didn't work.

The trend was spreading fast across tribes in other reservation and Quanah needed to use his influence to prevent Comanche and Kiowa become Ghost Dance followers. This practise had already led to the massacre at Wounded Knee, and the 'ghost shirts' worn during the dance had not protected them from the white man's bullets as the followers were led to believe. The practise was 'nipped in the bud' before it became riotous and deadly.

Public Domain Image

CATTLE BARONS AND FRIENDS

Flickr: Creative Commons
Licence/Commercial Use Allowed

Cattle Barons and Friends

Quanah's world in the cattle business became much bigger thanks to the cattle barons who continued to assist him in his quest for learning.

In time Quanah was able to build up his own herd of cattle, and learning and understanding the process of selective cattle breeding, until he was running nearly five hundred head of cattle of his own. Quanah soon became the supplier of beef to the reservation agency from his ever growing breeding herd.

From the very first time Quanah met him he had developed very strong bonds with Charles Goodnight and over time a huge friendship was built up with the Burnett family, working closely with them and learning as he went. But the friendship with the Burnett family was the strongest.

Public Domain Image
Samuel Burk Burnett

Samuel Burk Burnett, although the owner of a very large ranch with over 10,000 cattle, had a huge respect for the Native American. While other cattle barons were continuing to fight off Native Americans from 'their lands', Burnett understood and learnt a lot about Comanche and their ways. This knowledge he then shared, regarding the Comanche and their love of the land, with his own family.

The Comanche in turn showed their respect for the man gave him a Comanche name *Mas-sa-suta,* meaning 'Big Boss'.

Quanah had always been a 'people person' and had made many really influential friends, but out of all of his white friends Quanah held Burk Burnett as his greatest friend. He reportedly said **"I got one good friend, Burk Burnett, he big-hearted, rich cowman. Help my people good deal. You see big man hold tight to money, afraid to die. Burnett helped anybody."**

Quanah's high regard for Burnett showed when his family presented Burnett with his war lance and headdress.

Flickr: Creative Commons Licence/Commercial Use Allowed

With a growing herd and a small ranch of his own run by white men for him, he and his people were prospering. His holding consisted of a hundred and fifty acre farm that was watched over by a white man, two hundred hogs, three wagons, and one buggy (a light carriage pulled by a horse).

Quanah had real power now.

But the Dawes Act in 1887 (General Allotment Act) was to change all this. In simple terms, **"allows the President whenever he pleases to acquire Indians to give up their reservations for individual allotment."** This Act would affect a lot of tribes and cover 15 million acres of land.

This allowed the Government to break up tribal lands by making them into individual plots. In effect yet again stealing the land from the Native Americans, making them release their tribal land in exchange for a 'private parcel of land'.

"The objective of the Dawes Act was to assimilate Native Americans into mainstream US society by annihilating their cultural and social traditions." Wikipedia summary

They wanted the Native American to become farmers and ranchers it was as simple as that. To become like the white man, forget your heritage your traditions, and live the right way. It was a disaster.

Historian Eric Foner believed *"the policy proved to be a disaster, leading to the loss of much tribal land and the erosion of Indian cultural traditions."* The 'parcels of land' allotted to the Native American to farm on were usually parts of the desert where nothing would ever grow. Totally unsuitable and totally impracticable.

Between 1887 and 1934, Native Americans 'lost control of about 100 million acres of land' or about 'two-thirds of the land base they held in 1887' as a result of the act. The loss of land and the negative cultural effects of Dawes have since prompted scholars to refer to the act as one of the most destructive US policies for Native Americans in history. Wikipedia

This agreement would give the Native Americans 160 acres of land a piece and they could sell what was left over to the Government for $2 million with the individual land patents to be held in trust as non-taxable by the Government for 25 years.

Then unbelievably it got worse.

In 1889 President Benjamin Harrison appointed the Cherokee Commission, also known as the Jerome Commission after David Jerome, its chairman, to negotiate with the Cherokee and other Oklahoma tribes for their agreement to allotment and the sale of their surplus lands to the Government. Oklahoma Historical Society

The Commission's only purpose was to legally acquire land occupied by the Cherokee Nation and other tribes in the Oklahoma Territory for non-indigenous homestead acreage (the white man). Eleven agreements involving nineteen tribes were signed over the

Quanah Parker: One Man - Two Worlds

period of May 1890 through November 1892. ... Not all understood the terms of the agreements. Wikipedia

Quanah fought long and hard against this trying to get to the bottom of this agreement and where it would leave the Comanche, by badgering Jerome himself on the matter. Jerome tried hard to put delay answering Quanah but failed. Quanah was a man with a mission here. He had his people and his own livelihood to think of.

They were initially offered $1.25 per acre because the land was mainly rocky. Quanah however asked, *"I have noticed that coal is burned in such localities, and that iron, silver and gold are found in such places. The mountains are all supposed to be rocks and the rocks are supposed to be worthless, but the military use them to make houses with."*

But even such a good argument couldn't stop the progress that was wanted, and in October 1892 the Agreement with the Comanche, Kiowa, and Apache was signed.

Quanah signed this agreement although he would lose a lot more than any of the others as his $1,000 a year fees from his 44,000 acre pasture was lost, as this was originally leased to white cattlemen.

This agreement kept Quanah busy for the next eight years as he lobbied to try and change its terms. He wanted a new deal.

A deal where the Native Americans could keep all of their land and his efforts eventually paid off when 480,000 acres were set aside for this purpose.

Comanche weren't and never would be farmers. Their existence was fruitless. They had no purpose, no aims, and no goals. Not the Comanche way to live at all. Yes they kept enough land to live on with a house and maybe a few horses. But they had to resort to leasing out their lands to white men and living off the funds from the lease, plus any work they could get locally picking cotton or helping with the harvest. The Jerome Agreement was eventually altered to include 400,000 acres called the Big Pasture which was subsequently leased to white cattlemen. They were supplemented with about $100 in interest from the sale of the Big Pasture. The agreement became law in 1900.

New allotments were made in 1906 to all children born after the agreement receiving 160 acre parcels. All other remaining land was opened up to the white settlers, and this ended the Comanche reservation as it was.

But again the reservation became the place to be as about fifty thousand 'sooners' (a negative name for settlers) descended claiming the land regardless of any boundaries for the Native Americans and their parcel of land.

Soldiers from Fort Sill were sent to send them away but they always returned. And when they did they raided the livestock belonging to the Native Americans.

Nothing had really changed for the Comanche.

Quanah lost such a lot too now that the 'old Indian lands' had gone. The opportunity for earning the kind of money he had previously made had now gone.

And his generosity was his downfall too as he shared everything with the people who were constantly coming to see this famous Chief. And no one was turned away.

It has been said that Quanah's adopted white son Knox Beall said, *"My father fed a great many Indians. He had a great herd of cattle and horses in 1890 and when he died in 1911 he did not have many left because he was so generous. When a person became hungry he fed them. He could not stand to see any one of his tribe go hungry."*

A local store keeper apparently said of Quanah, *"By 1910, owing to his generosity and kind-heartedness, he was a very poor man. A great deal of his own food supplies were given away to his tribe and there were always hundreds of Comanche camped around his home . . . He was always kind, never speaking ill of anyone. And this man who once rode free on the high and windy plains had also lived long enough to witness the astonishing technological advances of the late nineteenth and early twentieth centuries. He found it all fascinating. He wanted to try everything. He had one of the first residential telephones in Oklahoma. He bought a car, an old ambulance for which he was ribbed by his friends, who called it a 'dead wagon', and which was apparently driven sometimes by his 'bodyguard', a deaf and dumb Comanche named George Washington, whom everyone called Dummie."*

But it didn't stop him. He was an influential man now and had many influential friends. And what better way to try to straighten things out was to talk to your influential friends. As it's not what you know, it's who you know as they say. So Quanah did.

One of Quanah's influential friends was President Roosevelt. Quanah had been invited along to his inauguration parade in 1905 and they had become firm friends. Quanah was invited to come up onto the stand with President Roosevelt and he was apparently invited to say a few words, although what was said is unknown. However, he is alleged to have said later that, **"I got more cheers than Teddy"**.

Public Domain Image

Public Domain Image

President Roosevelt was often invited along to Quanah's home called 'Star House' (his 10 roomed residence in Cache, Oklahoma) where he and many other influential friends would be entertained. Quanah had long since moved away from tipis.

In 1890, Star House was completed for Quanah to move into to. He had stars painted on the roof of the house (hence its name) because on a visit to Washington with Roosevelt he discovered that stars were very important to display rank for a General. So they were painted the roof of his two storey home housing ten foot ceilings, a formal dining room which had a lot of use, and a very large two storey porch. Star House still stands today and is worth much more than the $2,000 it cost then. Star House was paid for by his friends.

Quanah was well known for having an 'open door' policy meaning that no one was ever turned away. If they needed food or clothing, then Quanah would provide. Geronimo was another frequent visitor as they were firm friends too. Although Quanah didn't approve of Geronimo's appearances in Wild West shows.

Karen Reid (https://commons.wikimedia.org/wiki/File:Quanah_Parker_Star_House.jpg)
Quanah Parker Star House", https://creativecommons.org/licenses/by-sa/3.0/legalcode
Star House

Quanah tried to persuade his friend, President Roosevelt, whilst on a wolf hunt in 1905, with him and others, to try and discuss land issues that he wanted to keep for his people (particularly the 400,000 acres that the Government wanted for settlers).

They may have had a good time together at the wolf hunt but sadly Quanah did not win the argument. Not fully. Having said that the wolf hunt is said to have been the instigator for President Roosevelt to create the Wichita Mountains Wildlife Refuge on the land discussed in Cache/Lawton.

Flickr user jonathanw100. Derivative work: Diderot's dreams at en.wikipedia
(https://commons.wikimedia.org/wiki/File:Elk_Mountain,_OK.jpg)
Elk Mountain, OK, https://creativecommons.org/licenses/by/2.0/legalcode
Wichita Mountains Wildlife Refuge

It never put him off trying though. He was always a generous man sharing what he had with others and never turning anyone away if they needed help or food.

In 1902, at the age of around 57 years of age and to honour Quanah as their leader, they named him Deputy Sheriff of Lawton. Active even into old age.

Quanah continued his excellent leadership helping his people become self-sufficient and confident in their 'new life'. He continued to develop his people by building schools, planting crops, and everything to do with ranching and cattle rearing. His encouragement and support was never ending towards his people to learn the white man's ways.

Continuing his plan to improve Comanche life was the determination to give the children a good education. Comanche schools didn't make Quanah happy and the children were not welcome in the white man's schools. So he went lobbying for a new school district. In June 1908 after donating land to the school he became head of the school board for a district that he had donated the land for.

Public Domain Image

He became a judge on the tribal court and eventually established the Comanche Police Force which has grown to what it is today. Quanah believed that having their own police force would help his people to manage their own affairs. So that anything that had happened was dealt with and punished their way and not the way of the white man.

Public Domain Image

Public Domain Image

Comanche traditions were not totally forgotten by Quanah and he refused to adhere to the rule of one wife. He married two of his wives in 1872. His first wife was *Ta-ho-yea* (or *Tohayea*), the daughter of Mescalero Apache chief Old Wolf.

Quanah married her in Mescalero when visiting his Apache allies and bought her for five mules. But after being married for a year Ta-ho-yea asked if she could go back to her own home as she could not understand the Comanche language. So he sent her back.

His other wife from 1872 was *Wec-Keah* or *Weakeah*, daughter of Penateka Comanche subchief Yellow Bear (sometimes *Old Bear*). She was promised to someone else but love can't be beaten, and the two love birds eloped, taking several of the warriors with them. Yellow Bear was furious and gave chase to get her back. But Quanah made friends with him again and the two bands of Comanche joined forces instead of fighting over a woman.

Quanah liked women, and over the years, married six more wives: Chony, Mah-Chetta-Wookey, Ah-Uh-Wuth-Takum, Coby, Toe-Pay, and Tonarcy. Quanah Parker had eight wives altogether and twenty five children (some of whom were adopted).

It was said that he had been the wealthiest Native American of all time as at one stage he was reported to have invested in $40,000 worth of stock in the Quanah, Acme and Pacific Railway. But his constant generosity meant at the time of his death he had nothing left.

He fought also to keep the peyote tradition going as this had always been part of the Comanche culture, and was used for many other ailments too. He became the founder of the Native American Church Movement in the early 1900s, and peyote is regarded as a sacred and holy sacrament and is used as a means to communicate with the Great Spirit (God), also referred to as the Creator.

Public Domain Image

Quanah Parker's most famous teaching regarding the spirituality of the Native American Church.

"The White Man goes into his church house and talks ABOUT Jesus, but the Indian goes into his tipi and talks TO Jesus"

Quanah taught that the sacred peyote medicine was a sacrament given to the Indian tribes to be used with water when taking communion in a traditional Native American church medicine ceremony.

Peter A. Mansfield
(https://commons.wikimedia.org/wiki/File:Peyote,_the_pant.jpg)
https://creativecommons.org/licenses/by-sa/4.0/legalcode

It is said to trigger rich visual or auditory effects. But also and more importantly it was used by the tribe to alleviate toothache, pain in childbirth, fever, skin diseases, rheumatism, diabetes, colds and blindness.

But can be poisonous if taken in large quantities.

As the US Government became more involved in the control of drugs, the Native American Church faced possible legal issues regarding their use of the substance.

The Indian Religious Freedom Act of 1978, also called the American Indian Religious Freedom Act, was passed to provide legal protection for the Church's use of peyote

The controversy over peyote resulted in its legal classification as a controlled drug. Therefore, only card-carrying members of the Native American Church are allowed to transport, possess, and use peyote for religious purposes.

Quanah had worked hard and become a public figure. He was well known and a bit of a celebrity much like Geronimo his friend.

Geronimo is buried in Apache Cemetery, Fort Sill, on 437 Quanah Road. Unusual but rather nice.

Public Domain Image
Geronimo (left) and Quanah

But despite being a celebrity in the eyes of the US he was not an American citizen. He could sign treaties, be a Sheriff of Lawton, own land, negotiate with the white man, but he could not vote nor have any of the civil rights other Americans received. It was not until 1924, long after his death, that his children received US citizenship along with all Native

Americans when President Calvin Coolidge signed the Indian Citizenship Act making it law.

But the one thing that Quanah still wished to do was to bring his mother's remains from her grave in Texas, back to Oklahoma. He now knew where his mother and sister were buried, and managed to persuade congress to help him pay for their graves to be moved. His persistence paid off and a bill was passed authorising $1,000 to relocate their bodies.

The bill became law in March 1909.

Quanah travelled to Texas, meeting some of his white family, and found the cemetery where she was buried. On December 10th, 1910, she was re-interred at the Post Oak Mission in Cache.

At a ceremony over her grave, Quanah gave a simple speech, **"Forty years ago my mother died,"** he said. **"She captured by Comanche, nine years old. Love Indian and wild life so well, no want to go back to white folks. All same people anyway, God say. I love my mother."**

Little did he know but he himself had less than three months to live, as on February 23rd, 1911, Quanah died of rheumatism induced heart failure.

QUANAH'S DEATH

Public Domain Image

Quanah's Death

"Ladies and Gentlemen. I used to be a bad man. Now I am a citizen of the United States. I pay taxes same as you do. We are the same people now."

In February 1911, Quanah had been away visiting some of his Cheyenne friends whilst attending a peyote gathering. He was unwell. Perhaps even looking for a cure, through using peyote.

Travelling home by train with his number one wife, To-nar-cy, he sat on the train with his head bowed and lips apparently trembling. Once home he was taken straight to his house by his white son-in-law Emmet Cox. But the great man died.

On February 23rd, 1911 aged 66 at his home, Star House, Quanah succumbed to rheumatism-induced heart failure.

Word of his death moved like electricity through Oklahoma and Texas, in both white and Indian communities.

Public Domain Image

By morning hundreds had gathered at Quanah's house. By noon the crowd had swelled to two thousand.

Mourners came from far and wide travelling on horseback, farm vehicles or even cars. Not just Native Americans in their buckskins and bright blankets, but also Sunday best dressed white men and women came to pay their respects.

Quanah Parker: One Man - Two Worlds

They all moved in a long, slow procession to the church where only a small fraction of them could actually fit in. Those outside sang and prayed. Eventually they were able to pay their respects to a great respected man by filing past the casket where Quanah lay adorned in his favourite buckskin, his plaited hair falling over his shoulders.

Quanah Parker's body was buried at Post Oak Mission Cemetery near Cache, Oklahoma. He was only 66.

At the gravesite, mourners sang 'Nearer My God to Thee' and then the casket, draped with brilliantly coloured blankets, was lowered into the grave beside Cynthia Ann's.

Public Domain Image

In 1957, his remains were moved to Fort Sill Post Cemetery at Fort Sill, Oklahoma, along with his mother Cynthia Ann Parker and sister Topsana ("Prairie Flower"). The inscription on his tombstone reads:

> ***Resting Here Until Day Breaks***
> ***And Shadows Fall and Darkness***
> ***Disappears is***
> ***Quanah Parker Last Chief of the Comanche***
> ***Born 1852***
> ***Died Feb. 23, 1911***

When his family sorted through his estate, they found there was not much there. He had a few hundred dollars in the bank.

His wife To-nar-cy, who was recognized as his widow under Oklahoma law, took the rights to one third of his land allotment.

Wife To-pay, who had two children, aged two and eleven, got the house.

His eldest son, White Parker, received the now famous, photograph of Cynthia Ann that had hung over Quanah's bed.

Other than that there were a couple of horses and mules, a coach, a hack and buggy. He did not have much else left. He sadly was in debt for $350, a debt that was covered by the sale of his mules.

That was all that remained of the last Chief of the Comanche.

Four months after his death, the secretary of the interior ordered the Indian superintendent to eliminate the office of Chief and instead to create a committee formed of members of the tribes.

After his death he was replaced by a Chairman making Quanah Parker the Last Chief of the Comanche.

MEMORIALS AND LEGACIES

Public Domain Image

Memorials and Legacies

"Not only did Quanah pass within the span of a single lifetime from a Stone Age warrior to a statesman in the age of the Industrial Revolution, but he never lost a battle to the white man and he also accepted the challenge and responsibility of leading the whole Comanche tribe on the difficult road toward their new existence."
Biographer Bill Neeley

He was an important symbol of Comanche courage and pride. A force to be reckoned with and an individual that deserves great admiration and respect. He has mine already and many honours to prove that his memory will always live on.

Many memorials and honours have been bestowed on Quanah Parker. Many cities, highways, motels on southwest and north Texas once the land of the Comanche bear references still to his name.

He is even immortalised when he appeared in the first two-reel western movie ever made called **'The Bank Robbery'**, filmed near his home in Cache, Oklahoma. He had a bit part.

This is just some of the other tributes and honours to Quanah Parker.

The Quanah Parker Inn is located on US Highway 287 at the west end of Quanah, Texas.

Billy Hathorn at en.wikipedia
https://commons.wikimedia.org/wiki/File:Quanah_Parker_Inn,_Quanah,_TX_Picture_2189.jpg
Quanah Parker Inn, Quanah, TX Picture 2189, https://creativecommons.org/licenses/by-sa/3.0/legalcode

In 1970, Star House was listed on the National Register of Historic Places.

An exhibit describes Quanah and the Second Battle of Adobe Walls at the Hutchinson County Historical Museum in Borger, Texas.

The Quanah Parker Trail, is a public art project begun in 2010 by the Texas Plains Trail Region, commemorating sites of Comanche history in the Plains and Panhandle of Texas, the central region of Comancheria. Several places and buildings there were named after him:

The town of Quanah, Texas, county seat of Hardeman County is named after him. At the founding of Quanah, Quanah Parker made this blessing:

"May the Great Spirit smile on your little town, May the rain fall in season, and in the warmth of the sunshine after the rain, May the earth yield bountifully, May peace and contentment be with you and your children forever."

Nocona, Texas, is named after Quanah Parker's father, Comanche chief Peta Nocona.

'Empire of the Sun and Moon' written by S. C. Gwynne charts the life and times of Quanah Parker.

In 1962, Parker Hall, a residence hall at Oklahoma State University was opened and named in his honour.

The Quanah Parker Trailway (State Highway 62) in southern Oklahoma.

Quanah Parker Lake, in the Wichita Mountains, is named in his honour.

Quanah Parker Trail, a small residential street on the northeast side of Norman, Oklahoma Fort Worth. Along the banks of the Trinity River, is Quanah Parker Park.

The Quanah, Acme and Pacific Railway, which originated in Texas in 1902 and was merged with the Burlington Northern Railroad in 1981.

Quanah Parker Elementary School in Midland, Texas.

Quanah Parker: One Man - Two Worlds

2007, State of Texas historical marker erected in the name of Quanah Parker near the Fort Worth Stockyards Historic District recognizing his endeavours as a cattleman and Oklahoma rancher.

In 2019 the asteroid (260366) Quanah = 2004 US3 discovered on 2004 Oct. 28 by J. Dellinger at Needville, was also named in his honour.

The Quanah Parker Society, based in Cache, Oklahoma, holds an annual family reunion and powwow. Events usually include a pilgrimage to sacred sites in Quanah, Texas; tour of his "Star Home" in Cache; dinner; memorial service at Fort Sill Post Cemetery; gourd dance, pow wow and worship services. This event is open to the public.   Wikipedia

Jpo tx113
https://commons.wikimedia.org/wiki/File:Quanah_Parker_marker_and_statue.jpg
https://creativecommons.org/licenses/by-sa/4.0/legalcode

Memorial at Fort Worth

And not forgetting this book of mine to honour him ***'Quanah Parker: One Man-Two Worlds'.***

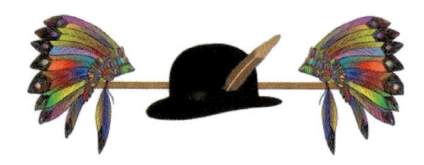

THE END OR THE BEGINNING?

Public Domain Image

The End or the Beginning?

He was a fighter and a good one. What can you say about this man that hasn't already been said? He was a rebel with a huge cause and hated for the 'white man' burned through his veins. Revenge was all he wanted.

The 'white man' had stolen the Comanche lands, decimated the major food source in the buffalo, killed his father, and captured his mother and sister who had both died in the white man's home of white man's diseases (influenza). He had every right to feel the way he did. Who wouldn't? What else could he possibly do but fight back and seek revenge?

But the change in him came gradually. He could see that *"It is useless for us to fight any longer, for the white man would kill us all if we kept on fighting."* He knew that they had to give in to a greater force. That the Comanche world, their way of life, was over. That things had to change. And quickly.

And they did. He was intelligent enough to re-invent himself into the 'white man's' world and see his second world opened up. A new start for his people too.

But his life had never been easy and it seems to have been built on conflict after conflict and continued to be a battle for new things over his later years, and all things to help and improve the way Comanche had to live now in the white man's world.

But it also gave him the opportunity of continuing to fight, in a different way without bloodshed, for his people.

And through the following years he was able to protect and care for his people. He became respected by the white man and his counsel was sought by not only Comanche people, but the white man too.

He really was 'one man-two worlds'. A force to be reckoned with and an individual that deserves great admiration and respect. He has mine already and many honours to prove that his memory will always live on.

I think that Quanah, if he were alive today, would be sad and upset to learn that around 90-95% of the Native American nations were lost during the white man occupation. Doesn't bare thinking about. It's horrific.

But the Native Americans in general, have started to fight back as many have become professional people, doctors, teachers, surgeons, business men and movie stars. My book **'The Footsteps They Left Behind'** tells the story of the massive progress made over the years, and the brilliant work completed already and the on-going changes and brilliant progress by Native Americans today. Quanah would be proud to see the changes now. Perhaps his experiences inspired future generations to make it big. The story of Quanah's life is told as part of American history in schools and colleges. I would like to think that even now his story still motivates and inspires young people. I hope so.

But we will and should all remember the Warrior Chiefs of yesteryear and honour their continuous fight to save their traditions and lifestyle. A battle we know that they sadly lost.

But moving forward, through an administration started during President Obama's time in office, the US government has agreed to pay a total of $492 million to 17 Native American tribes for mismanaging natural resources and other tribal assets, according to an attorney who filed most of the suits.

In a joint press release by the Departments of Interior and Justice, Secretary of the Interior Sally Jewel said, *"Settling these long-standing disputes reflects the Obama Administration's continued commitment to reconciliation and empowerment for Indian Country."*

The settlements mark the end of a push by the Obama administration to resolve, what the US says, is more than 100 lawsuits totalling more than $3.3 billion brought by Native American individuals and tribal governments against the federal government. The policy of reaching settlements on the disputes, some of which date back more than a century, is part of a campaign promise the president made to American Indians before he took office.   Wikipedia extracts

A popular Native American quote that says it all:

'Healing doesn't mean that the damage never existed
It means the damage no longer controls our lives.'

Quanah Parker: One Man - Two Worlds

Billy Hathorn
[https://commons.wikimedia.org/wiki/File:Quanah_Parker_photo_in_Shamrock,_TX_IMG_6163.JPG]Quanah Parker photo in Shamrock, TX IMG 6163", https://creativecommons.org/licenses/by-sa/3.0/legalcode

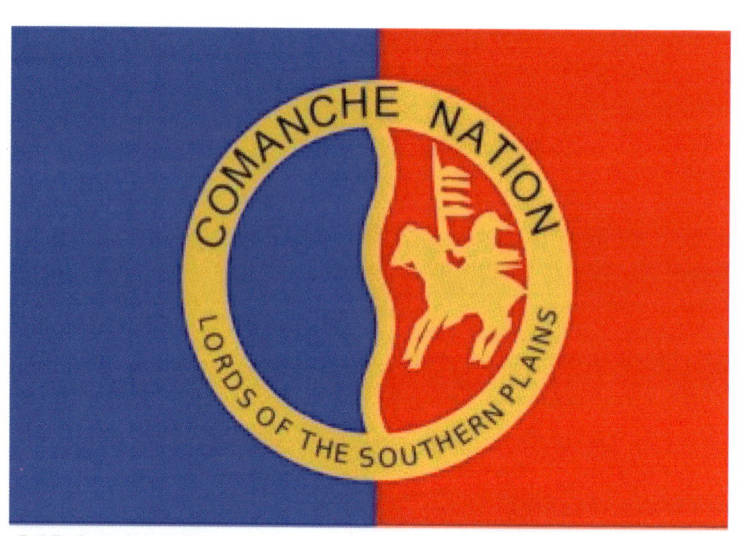

Public Domain Image

86

BIBLIOGRAPHY

BOOKS USED FOR REFERENCE

- *'Empire of the Sun and Moon'* written by S. C. Gwynne
- Native American Series – *'Comanche Life'* by Carol Dean
- Native American Series – *'The Footsteps They Left Behind'* by Carol Dean
- *'Where the Broke Heart Still Beats'* by Carolyn Meyer

WEBSITES USED AS REFERENCE

- https://en.wikipedia.org/wiki/Battle_of_Pease_River
- https://en.wikipedia.org/wiki/Charles_Goodnight
- https://en.wikipedia.org/wiki/Cherokee_Commission
- https://en.wikipedia.org/wiki/Comanche
- https://en.wikipedia.org/wiki/Comanche_campaign
- https://en.wikipedia.org/wiki/Cynthia_Ann_Parker
- https://en.wikipedia.org/wiki/Dawes_Act
- https://en.wikipedia.org/wiki/Fort_Parker_massacre
- https://en.wikipedia.org/wiki/Goodnight%E2%80%93Loving_Trail
- https://en.wikipedia.org/wiki/Herman_Lehmann
- https://en.wikipedia.org/wiki/Isatai%27i
- https://en.wikipedia.org/wiki/Native_American_policy_of_the_Barack_Obama_administration
- https://en.wikipedia.org/wiki/Nicholas_M._Nolan
- https://en.wikipedia.org/wiki/Peta_Nocona
- https://en.wikipedia.org/wiki/Quanah_Parker
- https://en.wikipedia.org/wiki/Quanah_Parker#Memorials_and_honors
- https://en.wikipedia.org/wiki/Rachel_Plummer
- https://en.wikipedia.org/wiki/Ranald_S._Mackenzie
- https://en.wikipedia.org/wiki/Second_Battle_of_Adobe_Walls
- https://en.wikipedia.org/wiki/The_Searchers
- https://en.wikipedia.org/wiki/Native_American_policy_of_the_Barack_Obama_administration

Quanah Parker: One Man - Two Worlds

IMAGES USED

Parker Fort - Page 3

Howitzer - Page 26

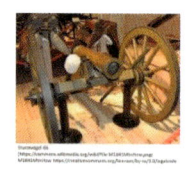

Peace Treaty - Page 27

Llano Escarpment - Page 30

Adobe Walls - Page 33 and 35

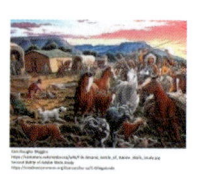

Palo Duro - Page 41

Adobe Walls Memorial Stone - Page 41

Quanah Parker: One Man - Two Worlds

Oklahoma and Indian Territories - Page 44

Charles Goodnight - Page 56

Star House - Page 89

Wichita Mountains Wildlife Refuge - Page 68

Peyote - Page 72

Quanah Parker Inn - Page 80

Memorial at Fort Worth - Page 82

Quanah Parker: One Man - Two Worlds

Quanah Parker - Page 86

Gordon Johnson from Pixabay - used throughout

Image by OpenClipart-Vectors from Pixabay - used throughout

Image by Clker-Free-Vector-Images from Pixabay - used throughout

ALSO AVAILABLE BY CAROL DEAN

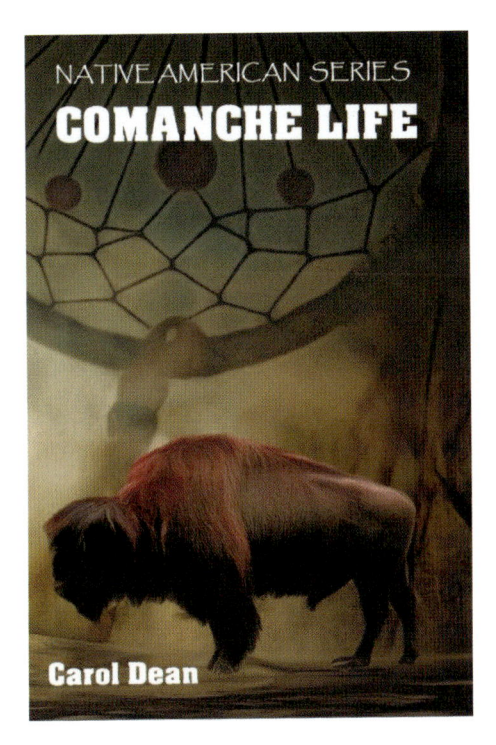

The Comanche were the fiercest and most feared of tribes. A warring tribe.

And a tribe, a people, fighting to preserve their traditions, values and the land they loved.

Find out how such a tribe lived their everyday lives, and how the Comanche almost fell into obscurity with the help of the 'white man', and how they rose again to be the Comanche Nation that they are today.

Available in hardback or paperback – black and white or colour.

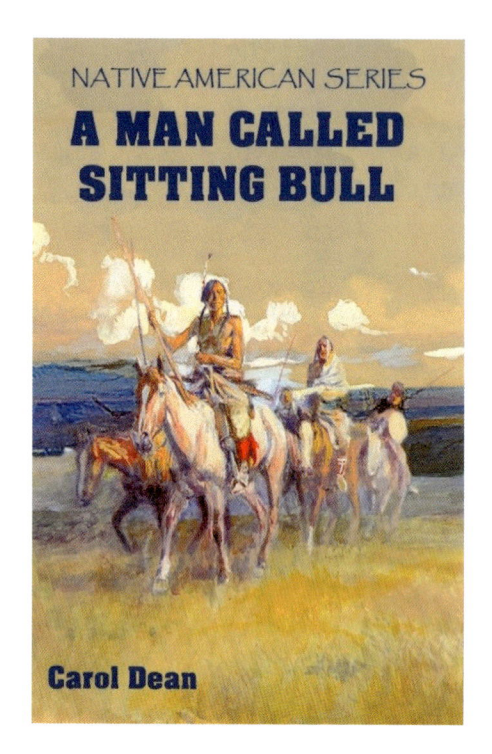

NATIVE AMERICAN SERIES
A MAN CALLED SITTING BULL
Carol Dean

Sitting Bull was born in 1831 in a time when the white man had descended on the Sioux tribal lands and claimed it for themselves. A turbulent time that continued throughout his life. A life of devotion to his family, caring for his tribe, courageous and brave in the face of danger and a gifted communicator with the animals and the Great Spirit.

His tribe held him in high esteem and spoke of his 'big medicine' which was a huge compliment to the man.

And that's only a small part of the man himself. Learn about the legend that was and is Chief Sitting Bull and perhaps you too will admire the man he became.

Available in hardback or paperback – black and white or colour.

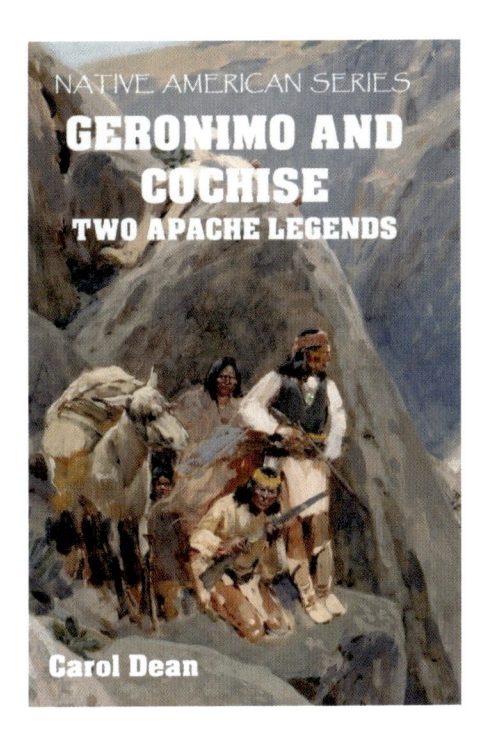

Over the years the Apache have been led by many legendary people. Two well known Apache legends, and the two that I have chosen to write about, are Geronimo and Cochise.

They lived in turbulent times. Times when these two legends needed to join forces to fight for their lands and the lives of their people against the Mexican and the American soldiers. Both forces seeking revenge and retribution for the deaths of loved ones at the hands of the white man's army, and the loss of their sacred lands desecrated by the white man.

Geronimo and Cochise's joint forces became a daring, dynamic and powerful fighting force to be reckoned with and feared.

This is their story.

Available in hardback or paperback – black and white or colour.

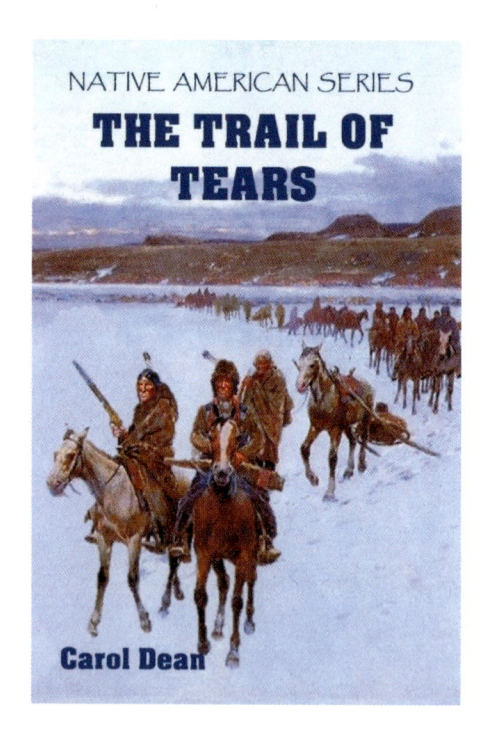

In the year 1830 President Andrew Jackson signed and had approved the Indian Removal Act. For the Five Civilised Tribes of Native America, the Choctaw, Chickasaw, Seminole, Muscogee (Creek), and the Cherokee, this meant the end of their lives as they knew it and the start of the Trail of Tears.

A trail that, not only brought tears, but has become famous for the starvation, disease, despair and death amongst the Five Civilised Tribes that were forced to travel on it.

An unbelievably sad story, said to be the most sorrowful legacy of the Jacksonian Era.

But it's all true.

Available in hardback or paperback – black and white or colour.

NATIVE AMERICAN SERIES

THE FOOTSTEPS THEY LEFT BEHIND

Carol Dean

When reading about Native Americans, not many will consider exactly what Native Americans are doing now. That's understandable considering the appalling history of battles for lands, traditions, and their cultures under the white man's hands. No set of peoples or civilisations have ever had to face such trauma as the Native Americans have for hundreds of years. That's the history that is read about, understood, and hopefully learnt from so that it never happens again.

But Native Americans have come through everything that they have had thrown at them over the years, and are now making a new history. A history of renewed interest and learning in their cultures, language, traditions, and their turbulent past. With many Native Americans reaching great heights in a very competitive world.

This book covers that new Native American history and honours just some of those involved.

Available in hardback or paperback – black and white or colour.

Printed in Great Britain
by Amazon